Free Rein

Racing in Berkshire and Beyond 1700-1905

Free Rein

Racing in Berkshire and Beyond
1700 – 1905

Penelope Stokes

Penelope Stokes

Published in the United Kingdom by

Penelope Stokes
The Holding, Hamstead Marshall
Newbury, Berkshire RG20 0HW
01488 658759
p.stokes@pop3.hiway.co.uk

First printed 2005

Copyright ©Penelope Stokes 2005

A CIP record of this book is available from the British Library.

ISBN 0 9528339 1 3

Contents

Introduction

Over the years of 1700 - 1900 Berkshire had a dozen racecourses operating at various times, all but two of them west of Reading. Within a 40-mile radius of Newbury there were another 28 in Oxfordshire, Wiltshire and Hampshire. Even allowing for the fact that they did not all operate simultaneously – perhaps only 15 of them ever had any semblance of continuity – Georgian and early Victorian race-goers were spoilt for choice. By 1900 however there were just two racecourses still operating in Berkshire, one in Wiltshire and none at all in Oxfordshire or Hampshire.

How did this come about? The story has been told at national level, with emphasis on the emergence of the premier-league courses whose names are familiar in the news today. Less well known is the tale of the also-rans, including those 30 or 40 racecourses around Newbury whose fitful fortunes reflected the ups and downs of local social history over nearly two centuries. The golden age of these country courses was the Georgian era; then came the cold draught of regulation, a more competitive environment and the railway revolution. The cull of country racecourses over the second half of the nineteenth century was ferocious.

Locality was the essence of these country race meetings: in the absence of mass communications they were festivals of local tradition, particular to individual communities. Most sporting history focuses on the heroics of the track, but this story concerns the people who underpinned country racing: the patrons, the organisers, the jockeys and trainers, the tradesmen for whom race week was a bonanza, the bookies and the ordinary people who walked or rode many miles to enjoy the spectacle and its sideshows. What did each of them get out of it? This book celebrates the life and death of Berkshire's country racing tradition, drawing on old calendars and almanacs, local newspaper reviews, diaries, maps, poetry, reminiscence and even sermons.

The geographical focus is on Newbury and west Berkshire, with occasional forays into neighbouring counties. Berkshire, for the purposes of this book, is Old Berkshire, before the Boundaries Commission transferred the northern third of the county into Oxfordshire. Old Berkshire takes in the White Horse, the Berkshire Downs, Abingdon, Faringdon, Wallingford and Wantage, as it was for about 1,200 years until the administrative reshuffle of 1974. However racing was not restrained by county boundaries, and the catchment area for a thriving racecourse could extend 40 miles, even in

Georgian times. This radius from Newbury is, therefore, the effective range of the story. Ascot obviously looms large on the edge of this area, but in this narrative it takes a back seat for two reasons: first, the nature of its royal foundation and patronage determined that Ascot was never truly a country racecourse; second, Ascot Racecourse already has the benefit of an excellent history written by Sean Magee.

The time span of the book covers the earliest recorded days of racing in the early eighteenth century, through the Victorian age and up to 1905, the date upon which the modern Newbury Racecourse was founded. From the outset this was a racecourse of the first rank and national importance, a status to which none of its predecessors in west Berkshire ever aspired. They were nonetheless the bedrock of a strong local tradition, the story of which is told here for the first time.

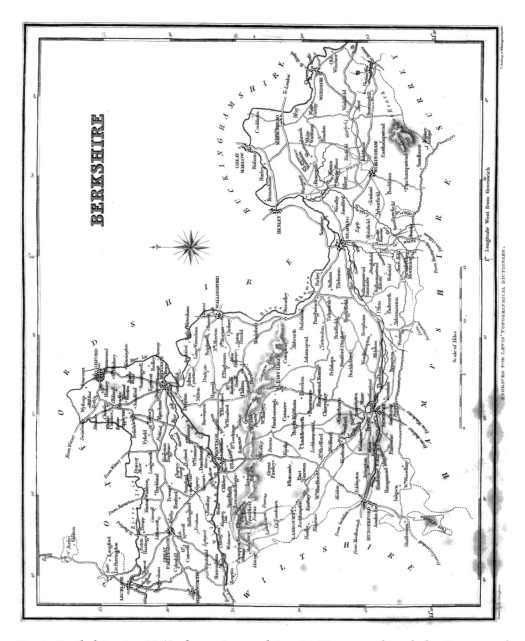

Fig 1. Berkshire in 1840, from Samuel Lewis' Topographical dictionary of England. Then (and until 1974) Berkshire extended northwards into the southern suburbs of Oxford, and included the towns of Faringdon, Wantage, Abingdon and Wallingford.

Acknowledgements

This book would have been much thinner without the generous help of Timothy Cox, who allowed me access to his vast of collection of racing books and materials, even when they were stacked around his house awaiting the building of the library extension. Now open to any *bona fide* researcher on application, the Cox Library is a magnificent resource for sport historians.

I would like to thank the staff of all the libraries, museums and record offices where other sources for this book were found: the Oxford University libraries of the Bodleian, the Department of Continuing Education, the English Faculty and the Sackler Library; West Berkshire Library; West Berkshire Museum; Reading Local Studies Library; Oxfordshire Local Studies Library; Berkshire Record Office; Hampshire Record Office; Rural History Centre (Reading); National Horseracing Museum (Newmarket).

I am indebted to others who answered various queries, sent me items of interest, agreed to the use of their illustrations and in one case even took me to the races: Les Corless formerly of the Tote; Paul Cannon formerly of West Berkshire Museum; the historians David Boyd and David Oldrey; the archivist of the Highclere estate Jennifer Thorp; the photographic historian Noel Chanan; Commander Rupert Craven; Peter Walwyn of the Lambourn Trainers Association; Gerald May.

Lastly, I would like to acknowledge that this project originated in a dissertation for an MSc at Kellogg College, Oxford, where I had the benefit of first-class tuition and guidance.

Penelope Stokes
The Holding
Hamstead Marshall
Newbury
Berks RG20 0HW

May 2005

Illustrations and credits

Front cover: An extensive view of the Oxford Races, by Charles Turner (1773-1857). Reproduced by permission of the Yale Center for British Art, Paul Mellon Collection, USA/Bridgeman Art Library.

Fig 1. Berkshire in 1840, from Samuel Lewis' *Topographical dictionary of England.* pv

Fig 2. Poster for Newbury Races 1815. Reproduced by permission of Gerald May. p4

Fig 3. The Upper Lambourn area from John Rocque's map of Berkshire, 1761. p8

Fig 4. The Ilsley Downs from John Rocque's map of Berkshire, 1761. p10

Fig 5. Fulwar Craven coursing at Ashdown, by James Seymour. p16

Fig 6. Benham Valence, by J. Nixon c1830. p17

Fig 7. Elizabeth Berkeley (1750 - 1828), wife of 1) the sixth Earl of Craven and 2) the Margrave of Anspach, by Ozias Humphrey. Tate, London [2005]; on loan to the National Portrait Gallery, London. p17

Fig 8. William Craven (1771 - 1825), seventh baron and first earl of the second creation, by Sir Thomas Lawrence c1802. p18

Fig 9. Oxford Races 1799, by Sartorius. From the *Sporting Magazine* (Dec 1799). Reproduced by permission of Timothy Cox. p31

Fig 10. Jockey Club of 1790, by Thomas Rowlandson. Reproduced by permission of Timothy Cox. p37

Fig 11. The Oxford to Southampton stage waggon. p41

Fig 12. A coaching supper at the Cross Keys in Newbury, by George Cruikshank snr. p42

Fig 13. as front cover above. p45

Fig 14. William (1809 - 1866), second Earl of Craven, by Comte D'Orsay, 1843. Reproduced by permission of the National Portrait Gallery. p63

Fig 15. William George Craven (1835 - 1906). From *Bailys Monthly Magazine* (June 1865). Reproduced by permission of Timothy Cox. p67

Fig 16. *Wild Dayrell,* 1855 Derby winner co-owned by Francis Popham and Lord Craven. Photograph by the second Earl of Craven. Reproduced by permission of Rupert Craven and Noel Chanan. p72

Fig 17. Park House yard, Kingsclere, in 1895. From *Racing Illustrated* (16th July 1895). Reproduced by permission of Timothy Cox. p76

Fig 18. Abingdon Racecourse mapped in the 1880s. Ordnance Survey first edition 1881-87. Reproduced from the CDROM *Berkshire Maps* published by the Berkshire Family History Society and the Berkshire Record Office. p85

Fig 19. Reading Races in 1844. From the *Illustrated London News* (September 1844). Reproduced by permission of the ILN Picture Library. p86

Fig 20. Ascot Racecourse mapped in the 1880s. Ordnance Survey first edition 1881-87. Reproduced from the CDROM *Berkshire Maps* published by the Berkshire Family History Society and the Berkshire Record Office. p88

Fig 21. Ashdown House, the Craven house near Upper Lambourn. p95

Fig 22. Windsor Racecourse mapped in the 1880s. Ordnance Survey first edition 1881-87. Reproduced from the CDROM *Berkshire Maps* published by the Berkshire Family History Society and the Berkshire Record Office. p96

Fig 23. Poster for Lambourn Races 1878. Reproduced by permission of Lambourn Trainers Association. p98

Fig 24. Advertisement for Hungerford's Rural Sports of 1881. From the *Newbury Weekly News* (24th March 1881). p102

Fig 25. Greenham mapped in the 1880s. Ordnance Survey first edition 1881-87. Reproduced from the CDROM *Berkshire Maps* published by the Berkshire Family History Society and the Berkshire Record Office. p103

Fig 26. John Porter, trainer of Kingsclere and founder of Newbury Racecourse. p104

Fig 27. Members of the Newbury Racecourse Company. From *Sporting Sketches* (3rd August 1905). Reproduced by permission of Timothy Cox. p105

Fig 28. Newbury Racecourse grandstand prior to opening day. From *Sporting Sketches* (3rd August 1905). Reproduced by permission of Timothy Cox. p106

1

'The equal of any county races in the Kingdom'
Georgian racecourses in and around Berkshire

Over the course of the eighteenth century a keen racegoer from Newbury might – transport permitting – have attended any one of between 30 and 40 racecourses within about 40 miles. True, not all these courses functioned every year. Abingdon, Ascot, Marlborough, Oxford, Reading and Salisbury were the longer-term stayers into the nineteenth century, but many others, such as Newbury, Hungerford and East Ilsley enjoyed fleeting decades of racing distinction interspersed with long periods of inaction. Others burst onto the racing scene for odd years here and there. For all racecourses, success depended upon aristocratic patronage, civic support, a healthy local economy and good communications. Rarely did all these factors combine favourably for any length of time, and even the most firmly founded racecourses experienced occasional lean years.[1]

Knowledge of the very early meetings comes down to us only incidentally because of a crime, or perhaps a royal presence. Datchet, near Windsor, hosted races for the entertainment of Henry VIII, and Salisbury is credited with racing in 1585.[2] A fatal stabbing caused the Burford meeting of 1620 to enter official records,[3] and a diarist mentioned Oxford's races at Port Meadow in 1630.[4] The foundation of Ascot Racecourse was the work of the monarch herself; Queen Anne designated a stretch of her own heathland for racing in 1711.[5] There was however no comprehensive listing of race meetings until 1727, when John Cheny issued his annual *Historical List of all Horse-Matches run, and of all plates and prizes run for in England*, which calendared race meetings and their results. After his death in 1750 the record was taken up by a succession of other publishers until 1772, when the Jockey Club licensed James Weatherby to publish the *Racing Calendar,* which remains the authoritative listing to this day.

---

[1] Appendix 2 tabulates the racecourses of Berks, Oxon, Wilts and Hants, giving details of their active years as far as can be determined.
[2] *VCH Wilts* vol iv p379
[3] STAWELL. *History of Burford and Bibury racecourse.* p6, 8
[4] CORDEAUX & MERRY. p56
[5] MAGEE. *Ascot.* p13

The early years of Cheny's list indicated a rapid increase in race meetings all over the country. Many of them were of dubious quality, which endangered racing's primary rationale: the improvement of bloodstock for military purposes. In 1740 Parliament passed a statute to limit race meeting numbers by introducing a minimum prize value of £50 per race. This was intended to eliminate under-funded events which might attract low-grade horses. The Act was never comprehensively effective (country fairs continued to hold horse races for prizes of harness or a flitch of bacon) but it immediately scotched numerous small meetings where £10 and £20 prizes had been the norm, including all the courses within a 40-mile radius of Newbury except for Reading, Oxford, Marlborough and Salisbury. However, after varying intervals most of the courses extinguished by the Act succeeded in drumming up the necessary prize money, and they returned to the calendar. Thereafter followed the heyday of country racing in the central south of England, lasting into the first quarter of the nineteenth century.

The early racing calendars listed racing at Newbury in 1738 and 1740 on Wash Common, a tract of corporation-owned common land on the southern edge of the town. Newbury then vanishes from the listings, but race meetings almost certainly continued, at least intermittently. Local historian Walter Money wrote in the Victorian era of 'racing on the Wash' in the later 1740s,[6] and the *Victoria County History* dates Newbury racing 'on the Wash' specifically from 1749.[7] Money also refers to military musters on the common, and their usual coincidence with racing. He describes a meeting and inspection of the 3rd Dragoons in 1777, attended by local townspeople in whom 'much curiosity was excited by the appearance of the drummers of the regiment, who were all black men'.

Newbury Races rejoined the official listings in 1805 as a new series. This was probably a relocation of the series that had just ended at Lambourn. From 1805 until 1811 two-day race meetings were held annually on common land at Enborne, owned by the Craven estate. The site was known variously as Crockham Heath and Enborne Down, but always calendared as Newbury Races. The flattish ground was conveniently close to the town, and the series was obviously successful. Cups and plates were sponsored by Newbury corporation and the Craven family. The *Reading Mercury* reported attendance by 'the rank and fashion of the county', for whom there was a grandstand. Ancillary entertainments both on and off the

---

[6] MONEY. *History of Newbury.* p336 and *Popular history of Newbury.* p103
[7] *VCH Berks* vol vii p308-9

race ground included prizefights, cockfighting, theatricals, ordinaries (which were special race-week *table d'hôte* menus at local inns), grand balls and parties. But in 1811 this land was earmarked for enclosure, ending the series. Newbury Races were then transported across the county border to Woodhay Heath in Hampshire, property of the newly succeeded second Earl of Carnarvon, friend of Lord Craven and supporter of racing at Enborne. Here the sport continued for a further three years. Little is known about the topography or indeed the exact location of the Woodhay course, except that newspaper reports spoke of 'the Craven mile' at meetings here.

The last meeting here, in 1815, was advertised in the *Reading Mercury* as scheduled to take place on Tuesday 13th and Wednesday 14th September. Entries were to be made at the Coopers Arms in Bartholomew Street, Newbury. The races, run in two-mile heats, included one for a £50 plate, and another for a £100 gold cup, although the donor was not named. The report following the meeting acclaimed its success, attended by a great many nobility and gentry, as well as some of the 'first sporting characters of the county'. 'Rare and costly viands and wines' were served at the ordinaries, Newbury's Pelican Theatre boasted never more fashionable audiences, and the Mansion House ball was crowded with 'all the neighbouring families of rank and fortune'.[8]

What the paper did not mention (nor indeed did the *Racing Calendar*) was a parallel meeting, also entitled Newbury Races, held on two days of the following week at Northcroft Meadow, an open space on the western side of town. Tuesday's three races were for 20, 10 and five guineas, for horses, galloways[9] and ponies respectively, to be run in three three-mile heats. Entries were to be made at the Anchor Inn. Wednesday's programme featured a pony race for which the prize was a saddle and bridle, and an ass race for one-and-a-half guineas run 'according to King's Plate Articles'. It is not clear from the poster whether this more plebeian festival was organized as part of Lord Carnarvon's Woodhay Heath meeting or as an entirely separate event.

---

[8] *RM* 20 Sep 1815
[9] In Georgian times the threshold between pony and horse was 13hh, and a galloway was a small horse of 13hh to 14hh. By today's definition the threshold between horse and pony is 14.2hh. The word galloway went out of use in the early twentieth century.

1815.

NEWBURY RACES.

TO BE RUN FOR

IN NORTHCROFT MEADOW,

On the 19th and 20th Days of September, at one o'clock in the Afternoon,

A Purfe of Twenty Guineas,

By any horfe, Mare, or Gelding that never ftarted for more than 20 Guineas—To run the beft of Three Three-mile Heats—Weight for Age—Three Years old to carry 8 st.—4 Years old 8 st. 9 lb.—5 Years old 9 st. 7 lb.—6 Years old 10 st.—Aged 11 st.—*Entrance One Guinea.*

THE SAME DAY,

TO BE RUN FOR BY GALLOWAYS,

A Purfe of Ten Guineas,

Not exceeding 14 Hands and an Inch—To carry Weight for Age.—The beft of Three Three-mile Heats—3 Years old to carry 6 st.—4 Years old 7 st. 7 lb.—5 Years old 8 st. 7 lb. 6 Years 9 st.—Aged 9st. 4lb.—*Entrance* 10s. 6d.

THE SAME DAY,

TO BE RUN FOR BY PONIES,

A Purfe of Five Guineas,

Not exceeding 13 Hands---catch Weights---to run the beft of Three Two Mile Heats---*Entrance* 7s. 6d.

SECOND DAY'S RACE.

TO BE RUN FOR BY PONIES,

A Saddle and Bridle,

The beft of Three Two-mile Heats---that never won a Prize---not exceeding 13 Hands high---*Entrance* 2s. 6d.

THE SAME DAY,

AN ASS RACE,

For One Guinea and a Half,

Free for any Afs---not lefs than fix to start---Riders to have one Spur and a Whip---no Stick or Boots will be allowed---nor yet Silk Stockings, or Jackets, or Caps, to run, according to the King's Plate Articles.

THE SAME DAY,

Will be run for as ufual, by *MAIDENS*, not exceeding 5 Feet 8 Inches high,

Four Holland Chemifes,

OR, LINEN CONVENIENCE OF LARGE DIMENSIONS, The fecond beft to have a Pair of excellent Cotton Stockings---the third a Pair of Excellent Scarlet Garters.

A Ham to be jingled for.

TO BE PLAYED FOR BY CUDGELS,

A Hat, Value One Guinea,

To the Man that Breaks moft Heads—each of the firft Ten Men that have their Heads broke to have Two Shillings each.—And other Amufements.

N.B. Horfes to be entered at the ANCHOR, NORTHCROFT-LANE.

MAYO, PRINTER, NEWBURY.

Fig 2. Poster for Newbury Races 1815. This event took place a week after the more formal Newbury Races held on Woodhay Heath.

In reporting the Woodhay Heath meeting the *Racing Calendar* promised another for the following year, but none took place. It seems that the shadow of enclosure continued to dog Newbury Races. The newspaper which reported the races also carried notices of enclosure meetings for Woodhay. The years following Waterloo were hard on agriculture, and from 1815 onwards the *Reading Mercury* carried many notices of rural bankruptcies and farms to let. The problems of finding a venue and sponsorship for relocating Newbury Races must have been insurmountable, and the town had no more calendared Flat racing until 1905. The fate of the more plebeian part of the programme is less clear. Such folk festivals probably continued at Northcroft, untroubled by the need for patrician support. Unfortunately they were considered too lowly for any formal record of them to be made.

Reading, with nearly twice Newbury's population (9,742 in 1801[10]), held calendared races from 1727 at various locations, settling eventually on the commons of Bulmersh Heath, which was owned by the old-established Blagrave family. Two-day meetings were held here annually, usually in late August, and starting at four pm to allow time for the innkeepers' ordinaries to be enjoyed at leisure from two pm. Meetings continued without interruption by the 1740 Act, when extra money was found to raise the prizes to the £50 statutory minimum. Later the series had its ups and downs. The course was vandalised in 1770, and in 1775 a riot took place after a dispute between mounted and pedestrian spectators. This event was commemorated in the local press by an anonymous poet who claimed to have been present.

> *The Heath resounded with a clatter*
> *Of whips and sticks which heads did batter*

Many people were hurt, and two rioters were sent to Reading Gaol.[11] Two years later the organisers advertised that 'the course will be put into very fine order', suggesting that facilities might previously have been lacking. A dip in attendance in 1788, when the meeting aspired to three days' duration, was attributed to the rival charms of spa towns, which had lured away the local gentry.

In 1814 the Blagraves sold Bulmersh Heath to a Mr Wheble, who subsequently enclosed it, although the location of the grandstand could still

---

[10] *VCH Berks* vol ii p234-43
[11] BOYD. *Running horses.* p11

be seen in the early twentieth century.[12] As with Newbury Races, the problem of relocating during the post-1815 agricultural depression extinguished Reading Races, at least for a few decades. They were dormant until 1843, when a new series relocated on King's Meadow.

Reading's supporters included two dukes of Cumberland, Lord Barrymore, John Elwes, Sir Charles Bunbury (president of the Jockey Club), the Leveson-Gower family of Bill Hill, the Mounts of Wasing Place and, of course, the town council. Eastern competition came from three courses on the edge of the county: Maidenhead held meetings from the 1720s until the end of the century on a course adjoining the notoriously lawless Thicket; Windsor had intermittent meetings during the eighteenth century, but this series had also vanished by 1800; Ascot, in the extreme east of the county, was more formidable, as a significant focus of royal and noble support. The meetings established here by Queen Anne declined after her death (Georges I, II and III having no great enthusiasm for the Turf) until the Duke of Cumberland revived it in the late 1740s. A second spell of doldrums followed the death of George IV, by which time Ascot was burdened with outdated traditions, and was failing to attract good prize money. However revival came with the advent of the railways, and the somewhat reluctant support of Queen Victoria. Thereafter the course moved into the premier league, leaving its western neighbours far behind.

Abingdon appears in Cheny's listings for 1730 and 1731, but then disappears until 1767. From then onwards annual meetings took place at Culham Heath (across the Thames in Oxfordshire) on a

> *course most judiciously laid out, both as a piece of fine racing ground, and also for affording diversion to the Company, as the horses may be seen quite round from an easy eminence.* [13]

The nearby city of Oxford was an additional reservoir of potential spectators, although the city had its own races at Port Meadow. As a parliamentary constituency, Abingdon races could command the support of its own MP, unlike other Berkshire courses, all of which had to share the favours of two county MPs. Lord Abingdon was the chief patron, supported by Lord Harcourt, the Craven family and John Elwes. Henry Pye, a Faringdon

---

[12] *VCH Berks* vol ii p309
[13] *JOJ Sep* 1767

landowner, politician and Poet Laureate, was another. Sir Charles Bunbury also raced here. By the late 1770s the meeting had expanded to three days, although this was pulled back to two in 1780. Attendance also dipped in the 1790s, as patriotic trippers chose instead to visit military encampments and ports mobilising for the French wars.

In 1812 the series relocated without a break to Abingdon Common. Here was a course of one-and-a-quarter miles, laid out as a flat, elongated oval, and soon to be graced with a grandstand built by the corporation. Abingdon seems to have weathered the post-Waterloo doldrums with relative ease; in 1817 *Jackson's Oxford Journal* declared that 'we may fairly presume the Abingdon meeting soon to be the equal of any county races in the Kingdom'.[14] 'The word 'county' is the key qualifier here, because by 1817 the rising importance of Newmarket, Epsom, York and Doncaster racecourses had already placed them in a league of their own. Goodwood and Ascot were later to join them. However Abingdon's unbroken run from 1767 to 1875 marks it out as the most successful of the west Berkshire courses.

Most of the also-rans lay in downland country, where they struggled in sparsely populated isolation. Faringdon never returned to the racing calendar after the 1740 Act, and Wantage, first calendared in 1727 and 1728, thereafter had only a brief run of meetings at Letcombe Regis in the 1790s. However Lambourn, where racing was first calendared in 1731, was active again within a decade of the Act on a course marked on the John Rocque map of 1761 at Row Down, half-a-mile south of Lord Craven's seat at Ashdown Park. Lambourn village, with only 2,045 souls,[15] could offer no civic support for prizes. Here were no assembly rooms for race-week balls, and transport links were abysmal. The racehorse training industry had yet to find its natural home on the downs. The village was so remote that few of Lambourn's eighteenth-century race meetings were written up in even local newspapers (although they were chronicled by the *Racing Calendar*). The course cannot have been economically viable, and its survival throughout the rest of the eighteenth century must surely have reflected Lord Craven's partiality for the venue. In 1803 however racing ended here, probably because an Enclosure Act for Upper Lambourn was introduced the following year.

---

[14] *JOJ* 23 Aug 1817
[15] *VCH Berks* vol ii p234-43

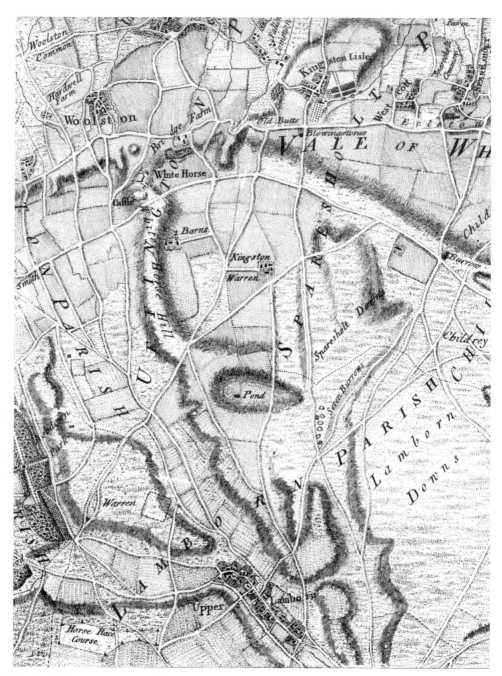

Fig 3. The Upper Lambourn area in John Rocque's map of Berkshire published in 1761. At the bottom left hand corner of the sheet a 'Horse Race Course' is identified. Lord Craven's Ashdown Park lies to the north of the racecourse.

Despite its tiny population base (512 in 1801[16]) East Ilsley was a busy centre with fortnightly sheep fairs throughout the summer, and through traffic on the main route from the midlands to the south coast. Communications were excellent. Race meetings were held here at Prestall Down near Kates Gore from 1727 to 1736 under the aegis of the Duke of Cumberland, after which the calendar suggests a long hiatus until 1804 when, for one year only, Ilsley stepped into the breach caused by Lambourn's demise as a racecourse. No further calendared racing was recorded at Ilsley until 1849. However official calendars may not give the full picture; both William Hewett[17] and Walter Money wrote of Ilsley's having an annual series in the late eighteenth century, and Money in particular claimed to have seen an engraved trophy testifying to this.[18] Like Newbury, Ilsley may well have hosted races which were too plebeian for inclusion in national calendars.

West Berkshire's smallest and most uncelebrated racecourse was at Bucklebury, between Newbury and Reading. It never featured in the *Racing Calendar*, nor in the sporting press, and the racers were certainly not thoroughbreds. Proof of the existence of the course has been bequeathed to us in the diary of Robert Bedding,[19] who in 1822 described a permanently laid-out racecourse on Chapel Row Common. It was used as part of the Chapel Row Revels, a robust annual folk festival with pony-racing as one of the highlights. The course was a bisected oval, over which races usually went round, up the middle, and round again, completing nearly two miles. Racing at the revels assumed more prominence after the 1830s when, following a fatality, the bloody sport of backswording[20] was banned. The decline of the revels and the extinction of Bucklebury racecourse were not documented, but probably came about in the mid-nineteenth century.

---

[16] *VCH Berks* vol ii p234-43

[17] HEWETT. *History and antiquities of...Compton.* p59-60

[18] *NWN* 8 Aug 1912

[19] HUMPHREYS. *Bucklebury.*

[20] Backswording was a form of cudgel-fighting in which combatants fought with one arm tied behind the back. Victory was usually granted when one contestant had drawn an inch of blood from his opponent's head.

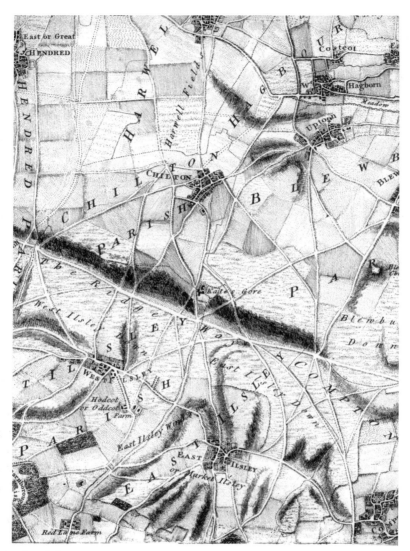

Fig 4. The Ilsley Downs in John Rocque's map of Berkshire, published 1761. Kates Gore is marked in the centre, at the foot of the Ridgeway. Today the name lives on only as Gore Hill, at the foot of which a petrol station on the A34 marks the former site of Kates Gore.

County borders may have carried significance for the magistracy and lord-lieutenancy, but landowners' interests, including racing, transcended them. Newbury lies close to Berkshire's southern border, and has always enjoyed strong links with Hampshire, where racing was well established at Stockbridge, Basingstoke, Odiham and Winchester by the late eighteenth century. Jane Austen was familiar with these meetings (and with those of Newbury) and made several references to them in her letters.[21] The Stockbridge course, situated just south of the Iron Age site of Danebury Ring, was a hilly, almost circular track, with the all-important straight mile. The view for spectators was superb. Always a fashionable meeting, Stockbridge enjoyed the patronage of the Prince of Wales and his notorious hell-raising friends such as Sir John Lade and Lord Barrymore. In 1831 it became the home of the Bibury Club, an ancient and exclusive racing society which moved there from Burford in Oxfordshire. Elsewhere in Hampshire there was sporadic racing at Alton (1740), Andover (1759), Horndean (1818), Portsmouth (1819), and Southampton also held intermittent series (1804 - 1810, 1822 - 1848). The regular patrons of these courses included the ubiquitous Cravens, Lord Portsmouth of Hurstbourne Priors, the dukes of Bolton and their successors, the Poulett family.

Nine miles west of Newbury lay the Wiltshire border, at that time running through the town of Hungerford. (The border has since retreated further west.) Hungerford was not to appear formally on the racing scene until the mid-nineteenth century, although uncalendared horse races were probably run on the common as part of other fairs and festivals. Marlborough, another 10 miles to the west, was an established and calendared meeting by 1730. The mile-long course on the common was renowned for its taxing uphill finish. Support for Marlborough Races came from the town corporation and local landowning families such as Brudenell Bruce (later marquesses of Ailesbury), Pleydell-Bouverie (earls of Radnor), Wroughtons, and the Pophams of Litttlecote. Marlborough's meetings prospered until 1811, when they transferred to Burderop, the seat of lord-lieutenant Thomas Calley near Swindon, for two or three decades. Racing also took place briefly at Cricklade (1813 - 1818), Chippenham (1808 - 1816) and Devizes (1835 - 1838). However Wiltshire's most famous and ancient racecourse was Salisbury, which survived not only the 1740 Act, but also enclosure, the agricultural downturn of the post-Waterloo period and the subsequent pressures of the Victorian era. Alone of all the country courses in the central south of England, Salisbury raced on successfully into the twentieth century.

Before the contraction of the northern boundary of Berkshire in 1974, the county extended northwards to the Thames, up to where it runs through what is now the southern part of the city of Oxford. Thus the Berkshire racecourse of Abingdon and that of Port Meadow in Oxford lay

---

[21] CHAPMAN. *Jane Austen's letters.* p204, 205, 235, 342-43

within a few miles of each other. Oxford Races first appear in a diary of 1630, when they were run annually on a two-mile, pear-shaped course.[22] A foreign visitor in 1710 declared Port Meadow's course to be superior to that of Epsom.[23] Meetings were supported by the city corporation, but they appear to have declined by 1767, such that the course was used for foot races and a pig-chase. The Duchess of Marlborough then stepped in with a £400 subsidy to upgrade the facilities.

Elsewhere in Oxfordshire racing took place at Burford, Woodstock, Chipping Norton, Banbury, Bicester, Goring and Henley, but none of these venues managed to sustain a long run.[24] By 1802 only Port Meadow was still in operation, and this meeting tottered after 1815. Despite support from the Churchill family and other notables, the meeting contracted from three days to two in 1817, and the 1819 fixture could muster only two runners for the Gold Cup. Nonetheless Port Meadow's racing endured until 1842, at which point it took a seven-year break.

A given of social history has it that race meetings were timed to coincide with local holidays, fairs and assizes.[25] However, this is questionable. Fairs and markets were important trading occasions, whose organisers would surely not have welcomed the diversion of their customers to the racetrack. Reading Assizes were held during Lent, when the racing season had yet to start, and Abingdon Assizes were held in July, although the town's races were usually held later in the summer. April to September was the favoured season for the more prestigious courses, and there was relatively little racing in October, the month in which both Newbury and Marlborough held their statutory hiring fairs. October and March were the last resort of less powerful meetings, such as Odiham and Andover.

A more pressing aspect of timing was the need to avoid a clash with other nearby meetings. All these venues were in close competition with each other for runners and spectators, although to some degree the downland courses (Faringdon, Wantage, Lambourn, East Ilsley) operated as alternative venues for what was essentially the same meeting. As the century progressed there is evidence of deliberate scheduling, although with so many venues in operation it was not always successful. The *Reading Mercury* complained testily in 1784 that Reading Races were unavoidably postponed because of a clash with Burford and Egham races[26] – a telling

---

[22] CORDEAUX and MERRY. p56
[23] HIBBERT. *Encyclopaedia of Oxford.* p331-2
[24] VCH *Oxon* vol ii p364-68
[25] VAMPLEW. *Turf.* p13, 135
[26] *RM 30* Aug 1784

announcement indicating that Reading's catchment area extended up to a radius of 50 miles. Maidenhead and Abingdon coincided in the first week of September in the same year, and Reading clashed with Newbury's opening meeting on 19th August 1805, after which Newbury Races drifted into September.

The preferred weekdays were overwhelmingly Tuesday to Friday. Sundays were protected by sabbatarian observance, and Mondays seem to have been unpopular. Saturdays were generally ruled out, being payday for farm workers. The extent to which racing encouraged absenteeism is debatable. In rural areas seasonal tasks were unevenly spread over the year and, outside busy times such as harvest, employers operated flexible working hours. In towns the time-work discipline was established earlier.

Day one of any meeting usually featured the big race, subsequent days being given over to lower-value races, more impromptu contests for farmers' hacks and ponies, and even non-equestrian events; the third day of Oxford Races in 1710 included a smock race, typically a foot race for young women, and always a popular spectacle. Half-a-century later the Port Meadow race programme also promised backswording, wrestling, pig-chasing and a sack race. The second week of Newbury Races in 1815 was also more of a rustic festival than a true race meeting.

Most meetings struggled with the constant uncertainty of future support. Racing historians have posited that one meeting per year was enough for any rural hinterland economy, because there was simply insufficient disposable income to support another, and this hypothesis is borne out by the local calendar. Lambourn experimented with twice-yearly meetings in the 1730s, but an advertised promise in 1737 of prizes for an extra early meeting the following Easter seem not to have materialised,[27] nor indeed did a similar promise of subsidy for Easter 1739.[28] Rather than schedule a second meeting, the more prosperous series tended to add on a third day, as happened at Maidenhead, Reading, Abingdon and Lambourn during the last quarter of the eighteenth century. By 1840 economic pressures had brought most country courses back to two days.

---

[27] CHENY. *Historical list.* 1737 & 1738
[28] CHENY. *Historical list.* 1738 & 1739

2

Patrons and their purposes
The personalities who made Georgian racing happen, and why

Until the mid-nineteenth century race meetings took place courtesy of the landed gentry as the main providers of runners, prizes, and often the venue itself. Most meetings were associated with a grand family name, the most influential of which in western Berkshire was Craven.

This family, originating from humble Yorkshire beginnings in the sixteenth century, had by 1700 acquired titles and 70,000 acres in four counties, not to mention extensive property in London. In Berkshire they owned 28,000 acres in the north and west, including seats at Hamstead Marshall, Benham Valence and Ashdown Park. Despite their vast wealth and potential influence the Cravens were by and large politically inactive, preferring to devote themselves to field sports. Fulwar Craven (1702 - 1764), the fourth baron and a noted racehorse owner-breeder, was a passionate example of the species. From his stables at Benham and Ashdown, his horses ran at courses throughout Berkshire, Hampshire and Oxfordshire. Fulwar himself founded the racecourses at Lambourn and Wantage and the Craven Hunt. He helped to found the Jockey Club in 1752, and membership was continued as a family tradition by the next three Craven title-holders. William (1705 - 1769) the fifth baron was also an owner, sponsor of races at Lambourn and steward at Abingdon, and continued mastership of the Craven Hunt. Next came the sixth baron, also William (1738 - 1791). He bred and owned racehorses, and supported meetings at Abingdon, Wantage, Lambourn and Andover. His racing interests however followed the trend of the later eighteenth century for first-class racing to gravitate to Newmarket, where he founded the Craven meeting in 1771. It is still a major fixture in the racing calendar.[1]

The sixth Lord Craven's wife Elizabeth (1750 - 1828) was equally keen, but her racing interests lapsed when the couple separated to conduct a long-running and acrimonious dispute about property and custody of their six children. After Lord Craven's death in 1791 she remarried, becoming the Margravine of Anspach (nowadays spelt Ansbach) and returning to Benham

---

[1] CRAVEN. unpublished family memoir.

Valence with her new husband and his extensive stud of racehorses. In his German principality the margrave was noted for offering his best stallions as sires to favoured tenant farmers – a gesture in keeping with the highest purposes of racing – but it is not clear whether he continued the tradition in England. Though no horseman himself according to Horace Walpole, he supported the newly founded Newbury/Enborne Races which started in 1805, but with his death the following year this support devolved upon his widow. The margravine had long maintained racing interests in her own right, to the extent that she qualified for inclusion in a savagely satirical publication of the 1790s entitled *The Jockey Club or a Sketch of the Manners of the Age,* (Pigott) which mercilessly lampooned her high self-regard and theatrical ambitions. Benham Valence was furnished with an outdoor theatre for the entertainment of her racegoing visitors, and here the margravine starred in productions of her own composition. Her sense of theatre was carried into all aspects of her public life, not least her arrival at and departure from racecourses.

Fig 5. Fulwar Craven coursing at Ashdown. This mid-eighteenth-century painting by James Seymour depicts the downland landscape of Upper Lambourn, with the Craven seat of Ashdown House just visible in the far distance.

Fig 6. Benham Valence, engraved from a drawing by J. Nixon c1830. The house and park remained in Craven hands until the mid-nineteenth century.

Fig 7. Elizabeth Berkeley (1750 - 1828), wife of 1) the sixth Earl of Craven and 2) Margrave of Anspach, by Ozias Humphrey. Racehorse-owner and supporter of Newbury Races.

The margravine's son the seventh baron William (1771 - 1825) served with distinction as ADC to the Prince of Wales in the French wars, and thus he regained the defunct family earldom in 1801.[2] He lived at Ashdown House, where he kept racehorses (and, according to Jane Austen, a mistress). He was an active member of the Jockey Club, and supported race meetings on Craven land at Lambourn. These came to an end in 1803, probably because enclosure of the ground was planned. It is also possible that the earl thought a racecourse sited nearer Newbury might be more successful. If so, he was right. The Newbury Races on Craven land at Enborne Heath from 1805 - 1811 were indeed popular.[3]

Fig 8. William Craven (1771 - 1825), seventh baron and first earl of the second creation, by Sir Thomas Lawrence c1802. Racehorse owner and breeder, member of Jockey Club, steward at Abingdon, supporter of racing at Lambourn, founder of racing at Newbury/Enborne 1805-1811.

---

[2] The first earl, William Craven (1608-1697), died without issue, and thus the earldom lapsed, leaving only the barony to pass down future generations. The revival of the earldom in 1801 made William Craven (1771-1825) technically the first earl of the second creation.

[3] The Craven family's involvement in racing is summarised in Appendix 1.

North of Newbury William Augustus, Duke of Cumberland (1721 - 1765) rented an estate at Kates Gore in East Ilsley where, in the 1730s, he established a stud and a racecourse. Following his notorious suppression of the Jacobites at Culloden in 1745 he was made a Ranger of Windsor Forest, after which most of his racing interests transferred to Ascot, but Kates Gore was still maintained as a ducal racing establishment. Local legend has it as the birthplace in 1764 of the legendary winner and sire *Eclipse*, but the same honour is claimed more plausibly for Cranbourn Lodge in Windsor Great Park, where a stone commemorates the event. However, if not foaled near Newbury, *Eclipse* certainly trained on the Ilsley downs as a yearling, as did the equally famous *Herod*.

Following the duke's death in 1765, East Ilsley's racing history becomes obscure. W. J. Hewett, writing in 1844, states that the future George IV wished to buy Kates Gore, but that the landlord, a Mr Head, razed the premises rather than sell to the royal family, because the duke's servants had behaved badly.[4] This account overlooks the anomaly that the future George IV was but two years old at the time of the first Duke of Cumberland's death, so would have been an unlikely prospective purchaser. Nor was his father, George III a plausible candidate, as he shared the early Hanoverian monarchs' indifference to racing. It is however possible that Cumberland's nephew and successor to the dukedom, Henry Frederick (1745 -1790), took over Kates Gore. Certainly this second duke had runners at Abingdon races in 1767, and at Winchester and Andover in 1777. The demolition of the house and stables may have taken place after his death but, notwithstanding this, an East Ilsley racecourse definitely operated in 1804, and again in the mid-nineteenth century. By the late nineteenth century it was but a dim memory, although locals still referred to a barn as the 'rubbing house', a noted feature of Georgian racecourses.

Several generations of the Bertie family (earls of Abingdon) directly sponsored Abingdon and Oxford races, in addition to supporting those at Wantage and Lambourn. Willoughby Bertie (1740 - 1799), the fourth earl, was the most active in racing patronage. In 1770 he had a white horse figure cut into the chalk down of Westbury, perhaps in emulation of his friend Lord Craven, who owned the original White Horse of Uffington. Following a fire, the Bertie country seat of Rycote, near Thame, was lavishly restored during the 1770s in the style of a Renaisssance palace. Capability Brown designed the gardens, and no expense was spared in building racing stables and paddocks, some of which still appear on twentieth-century maps. An ardent

---

[4] HEWETT. *History and antiquities of the hundred of Compton in Berks.* p59-60

huntsman, Lord Abingdon founded the Earl of Abingdon's Hunt, and frequently rode his own horses on the racetrack. He kept a stable at Newmarket,[5] but it was at Rycote in 1773 that he bred *Pot8os*, a famously successful horse. However, in selling the stallion to Lord Grosvenor during the course of a race (the price being a gamble on the outcome) Lord Abingdon robbed himself of the £61,971 stud fees which *Pot8os* went on to earn after his successful racing career.[6]

In additional to racing interests Lord Abingdon had intellectual accomplishments, being a distinguished poet, flautist, composer, and friend of Haydn and J.C. Bach. In politics he was an active radical in the House of Lords, supporting John Wilkes, the American rebellion and the French Revolution. But, in keeping with the traditions of his age and class, he bet heavily and this, compounded by his generally lavish lifestyle, led inevitably to financial difficulties. In 1778 he published a poetical *Adieu to the Turf* addressed to the Archbishop of York, forswearing all racing activities. It was surely tongue-in-cheek, because the following year finds Lord Abingdon at Newmarket, short of the 3,000 guineas required ante-post for a celebrated match against Lord Grosvenor; he was obliged to accept a loan from his friend John Elwes.[7] Lord Abingdon was the winner, but seemingly the rewards did not suffice to arrest his financial decline. When he died at Rycote in 1799 the asset-stripping which he had been forced to initiate was enthusiastically continued by his successor the fifth earl, although the family managed to sustain a degree of racing interest. Little of Rycote remains today. The house was sold off and demolished in 1807, although the site was the focus of an archaeological investigation around the turn of the millennium.

The afore-mentioned John Elwes (1714 - 1789) of Marcham Park, in the north-west of the county, was dubbed the 'Berkshire miser'. Charles Dickens referred to him in *Our Mutual Friend,* and he featured in *Merryweather's Lives and Anecdotes of Misery.* His name was a byword for self-inflicted penury, but his character seems to have been rather more complex. The roof of Marcham Park may have leaked, but Elwes was a considerate landlord to his tenants. He never took a coach, preferring the cheaper option of horseback (cross-country, dodging turnpikes), but he cared keenly for good horses and foxhounds. When travelling he carried a boiled egg in his pocket to avoid expenditure on food, yet he was said to be

---

[5] MINGAY. *English landed society.* p151
[6] TAUNTON. *Famous horses.* p50
[7] MORTIMER. *Jockey Club.* p55

a connoisseur of French food and wine. He never cleaned his shoes, wore a wig found in the gutter, and never married the housekeeper who bore his two children, but he provided dutifully for them on his death. Gambling was his only extravagance, and he made generous loans to his racing friends. 'Painfully anxious to keep his own, he never panted for the wealth of another' was his epigraph from the *Gentleman's Magazine*.[8] A steward at Abingdon and Maidenhead races, he was probably more principled than many of his contemporaries.

A notorious rake and hell-raiser of eastern Berkshire was Richard Barry (1769 - 1793), seventh Lord Barrymore, an Irish peer with an estate at Wargrave-on-Thames. A one-time friend of the Prince of Wales, he lived riotously, reputedly spending £300,000 in his short racing career as owner, gambler and jockey. In debt before his majority, he borrowed to build a private theatre at Wargrave for the entertainment of his racing guests. His notoriety as a gambler was enhanced by the much-repeated tale of his wager that he would eat a live cat, although sources differ as to whether or not he actually performed the deed. Caroline Lybbe Powys, a diarist of gentle family owning substantial estates in Oxfordshire and Berkshire, and an avid racegoer, was charmed to find herself in his company at the Reading Races ball,[9] but not everyone held him in such high regard. As a candidate for Reading in the 1791 election he polled only 44 out of 562 votes. It was said that when he was appointed steward of Reading Races the fixture was shunned by mainstream racing support, such that he was obliged to enter his own horses under his friends' names.[10] As one of 'Prinny's set', Barrymore devised amusements such as the Four-in-Hand Club, whose members would commandeer a stage coach, complete with terrified passengers, and drive it recklessly until they either crashed or tired of the diversion. In 1791 Barrymore fell out with the Prince of Wales. Subsequently he laid out 1,700 guineas on two banquets at Ascot in the hopes of rekindling the prince's friendship but alas, his ostracism was complete, and the invitations were ignored by one and all. Two years later Barrymore died, aged 23 and newly married, in a gun accident.

The Prince of Wales (1762 - 1811), later Prince Regent (1811 - 1820) and eventually George IV (1820 - 1830), took an interest in racing soon after his majority in 1783. Supposedly encouraged by his uncle the second Duke of Cumberland, he bought, bred and raced horses such that within four

---

[8] *Gentleman's Magazine* lix p905
[9] POWYS. *Passages from the diaries.* p226
[10] *Truth as opposed to fiction...Barrymore.* p75

years Parliament had to vote him £161,000 to redeem his debts. His stable was said to be the finest in the country, although he lacked big-race winners. In a scandal known as the *Escape* Affair at Newmarket in 1791, the prince's horse performed badly, and then won soundly the next day at five to one. The jockey, Sam Chifney, was suspected of pulling, and the prince was warned by the Jockey Club not to continue to employ him. The royal riposte was to grant Chifney a handsome annuity, and the prince never again attended Newmarket, nor had any further dealings with the Jockey Club. Instead, his attentions turned to the Bibury Club (then at Burford), where races were confined to gentleman members who usually rode their own horses, under their own rules. In addition to racing with the Bibury Club however, the prince also attended Stockbridge and Banbury races. It is quite likely, although not recorded, that he attended other racecourses around Newbury. He certainly made regular visits to various hunting friends in the area: the Brudenell Bruces near Marlborough and the Cravens at Benham, not to mention the home of his former tutor, the eccentric Stephen Poyntz at Midgham, whose estates and hounds were maintained solely for the prince's fox-hunting pleasure.[11]

Other grand families who supported local racing at this time included the Wroughtons of Woolley Park, the Pyes of Faringdon, the Throckmortons of Buckland, and the Dundas family of Kintbury. In Wiltshire the Pleydell-Bouveries (earls of Radnor) supported Marlborough, Burderop and Salisbury races, but they also had strong Berkshire interests. Just south of Newbury across the Hampshire border lay the Highclere estate of the Herbert family (earls of Carnarvon), to which the Newbury Races transferred after Enborne Heath was enclosed in 1811. Lord Portsmouth lived at Hurstbourne Priors to the south-west and the Pouletts (dukes of Bolton) at Hackwood Park, the venue for Basingstoke Races. All these families to the south of Newbury were owner-breeders, supporting Newbury and Reading in addition to the Hampshire courses of Stockbridge, Basingstoke, Odiham and Winchester.

The grand families of racing were interlinked by marriage, military connections, hunt membership, public service as lord-lieutenant, MPs, JPs, high stewards and sheriffs, and all the complex networks of upper-class society. At each other's meetings they gathered for a variety of convivial and practical purposes; land deals were contracted, loans granted, politics fixed, appointments secured and marriages arranged. Such transactions depended

---

[11] AESOP. *Sporting reminiscences in Hampshire.*

upon a dutiful turnout of county families, making racegoing a social obligation as much as a chosen sporting pursuit. Most west Berkshire meetings drew the landowning society from a radius of about 40 miles, embellished by a few noblemen of national significance who happened to have local seats. Such a distance was considered quite feasible for racing attendance by those on horseback or perhaps by carriage if ladies were present. Thus the Duke of Bolton would travel from Winchester, and Lord Barrymore from Wargrave, to Newbury Races. However, a description of East Ilsley Races eulogising the venue as 'a trysting place for representatives of the nobility, gentry and commonalty who had the means of getting thither from every part of the kingdom'[12] sounds like optimistic hyperbole. No racecourse of the eighteenth century could aspire to a national catchment.

Whilst the gentlefolk might ride, the racehorses themselves had to be walked to meetings. This was time and energy consuming, and entailed the risk of injury on route. Thus the record of horses such as the Hampshire-bred *Gimcrack,* which raced at Ascot, Marlborough, Odsey, Wantage, Wells and Wisbech all in the 1767 season, was both remarkable and exceptional.[13]

Most of the admirals, generals, MPs, nabobs and landed gentry attending Newbury and surrounding country racecourses were therefore of county rather than national significance. Race meetings afforded an opportunity for this local governing class to assert its primacy over the masses in a good-natured, paternalistic fashion. Here was a classic example of the 'theatre of authority' described by the historian E. P. Thompson, in which the labouring and middling sorts witnessed a show of power by their betters. According to Lord Willoughby de Broke there was a fixed order of precedence within Georgian county society: the lord-lieutenant occupied pride of place, followed by the Master of Fox Hounds; major landlords outranked the bishop, who in turn could look down upon the chairman of Quarter Sessions; behind these trooped members of Parliament, deans, archdeacons and magistrates respectively.[14] It was customary for the races to be preceded by a grand parade of the élite in their finery, an entertaining but also purposeful spectacle of wealth, clothes, horses and retinue. Contemporary reports of Newbury's Enborne Races of 1811 detailed many lords and ladies and their equipage, giving particular prominence to the Margravine of Anspach, who processed from nearby Benham Valence with

---

[12] Walter Money writing in *NWN* 8 Aug 1912 quoting 'a contemporary sporting scribe'
[13] MAGEE. *Ascot.* p28
[14] CANNADINE. *Decline and fall of the English aristocracy.* p356

'scores of grooms as radiant as new liveries and old ale could make them'.[15] The margravine's son, the Earl of Craven, followed with his countess and a splendid retinue. William Poyntz, son of Stephen the tutor to the Prince Regent, drove over from Midgham with a large party in a carriage-and-four with outriders and positilions.[16] Also were noted the beautiful greys of Matthew Montagu (who had inherited Sandleford Place from his aunt, the celebrated bluestocking Elizabeth Montagu), the equally fine bays of Anthony Bacon, a local landowner credited with raising an entire company for the Berkshire militia in 1799. The races, incidentally, provided fertile recruiting ground for the military during the French wars; the second day of Abingdon races in 1797 was used to rally support for the Berkshire Volunteer Corps.[17]

Race meetings have been credited with a wider social function in permitting a class mix which was unobtainable in other social spheres. It is doubtful that vertical class relations were seriously subverted, but there was certainly a carnival atmosphere, and the gentry would often come down from their exclusive grandstands to mingle with the crowd. An air of licence allowed the upper classes to ignore some conventional constraints, behaving in a fashion which would not have been tolerated in drawing-room society. A nobleman might take his mistress rather than his wife to the races. The Duke of Grafton flaunted Nancy Parsons at Ascot in 1764,[18] and one of Lady Craven's many complaints about her husband the sixth baron was that the mistress he took to Reading Races dared to pass herself off as Lady Craven. Elizabeth Chudleigh, Countess of Bristol and later (bigamously) the Duchess of Kingston, planned her elopement at Winchester Races. Notwithstanding such scandals respectable Georgian ladies could attend without compromising their reputations. The roll call at Enborne in 1811 specifically mentions several peers' wives, and one Lady Jane Man apparently unaccompanied.

'An Englishman would almost as soon think of the prime minister turning mountebank as that a race meeting would be made the nucleus for a political or revolutionary purpose' according to an anonymous nineteenth-century writer,[19] and indeed historians have pointed to the untroubled

---

[15] MONEY. 'Newbury races in the old days.' *RM* 18 Nov 1922 p8
[16] *RM 19* Aug 1811
[17] *JOJ* 9 Sep 1797
[18] MAGEE. *Ascot.* p28
[19] *Horse racing: its history and early records of the principal and other race meetings.* p15

atmosphere at Manchester races shortly after Peterloo as an example of the social stability of racing crowds.[20] The racecourse drew together aristocrats of opposite political persuasions, such as Wroughtons and Pyes, who were Tory, and Lords Craven and Abingdon who were not only Whig, but fervent supporters of the American rebel colonists to boot. That the ruling classes used race meetings for political fixing is apparent from a row that reached the pages of *Jackson's Oxford Journal* in 1770, when a prospective parliamentary candidate reneged upon a deal made at Abingdon Races: 'Did you not at the last Races, at Abingdon, give your word of honour that you would not oppose Mr Bayly in the next General Election?' wrote the outraged correspondent.[21] The memoirs of Rupert Craven note that two years later the sixth Lord Craven and his friend Lord Abingdon were instrumental in getting John Elwes into Parliament as MP for Berkshire. It is not difficult to imagine this too being arranged at Abingdon Races, where all three were habitués. General elections in Banbury made use of the town's racing tradition, with both candidates (one of them a Pye) publicly vying for primacy in their racing subscriptions in 1832. However most of this may have gone over the heads of the general public. The *Oxford University and City Herald* reported that 'an attempt was several times made [at Banbury Races 1832] to set up a cry of "Pye for ever!" in which that gentleman's servants joined most lustily. The attempt however completely failed.'[22]

Many aristocrats at least dabbled in racehorse ownership. Financial gain was certainly not a motive because then, as now, ownership was rarely remunerative. Some owners have been credited with patriotism, supporting the royal policy of improving bloodstock for military purposes, but when this principle was eroded by shorter, faster races and less robust racehorses there was no immediate decline in the enthusiasm of noble patrons. Prestige was almost certainly a larger factor. Although horses frequently changed hands, the truly dedicated Turfites liked to breed their own winners, reassured perhaps by the successful outcome of carefully considered pairings not unlike their own marriages.

Racehorse ownership, and the heavy betting which went with it, was traditionally the pursuit of renegade high-born sons, the Prince of Wales being the archetype. Training, transport, farriery, saddlery, stabling away from home, entry fees and forfeits, watchmen and walkers combined to

---

[20] BAILEY. *Leisure & class in Victorian England.* p23
[21] COX. *Story of Abingdon pt VI: eighteenth-century county town.* p135
[22] BROWN-GRANT. p26-31, 68-79

drain the most robust family fortune. Race prize money (£50 was the norm for most races at Georgian country courses) was swiftly dissipated on obligatory gifts to racecourse officials, celebrations, and rewards for loyal retainers. The funding of ownership was therefore dependent upon betting, which frequently multiplied debts rather than meeting them. This was the age of 'plungers': young noblemen who achieved notoriety for heroic losses at the race track.

Whilst some female owners raced under their husbands' names quite a few scorned such timid shelter; at the founding meeting of Ascot in 1711 Queen Anne ran horses under her own name, on her own course and won her own Queen's Plates. The Margravine of Anspach raced under her own name at Newbury, as did Lady Bampfylde at Stockbridge and Reading, the Duchess of Marlborough at Oxford, the Duchess of Kingston and Lady Catherine Poulett at other Hampshire courses. At Newbury's first meeting in 1739 'there being nothing that would run against Mrs Jones' grey mare, *Why Not,* the town generously gave her five guineas, returned her entrance, and the prize not run for.' [23]

Whilst most racehorse owners were upper-class, there was the odd exception; John Alder, a publican of Abingdon, won first prize in the state lottery of 1767. He spent his winnings on a horse called *Sulphur*, which won at Abingdon in 1768, and was subsequently bought by the second Duke of Cumberland. [24]

Landowners might appear to have been the driving force behind country racing, but urban wealth also played an active and important part. Most meetings also depended upon the local town council for sponsorship, and where the course was sited on council-owned land, the council was pre-eminent. Such was the case for the earliest series of Newbury Races. Having bought the site of Wash Common from the Crown in the seventeenth century, Newbury town council was the principal organiser of the calendared races of 1739 and 1740, and probably also of other uncalendared meetings earlier and later in the century. The series of 1805 to 1811 took place on Craven land at Enborne Heath, but the council still voted to fund a corporation cup worth £50. Until 1811 Abingdon Races were held on Culham Heath, for which the corporation regularly debated the appropriate level of its support. In 1733 it was 10 guineas for a galloway plate, rising to £30 towards a £50 purse or plate in 1767. At one time support was briefly withdrawn altogether, suggesting that approval for racing was by no means

---

[23] *RC* 1739
[24] HOOKE. *Abingdon, Berks.*

unanimous, although the ban did not last. When the races transferred to Abingdon Common in 1812 the town council built a grandstand. Village-based courses such as Lambourn and East Ilsley struggled to survive without patronage from this kind of civic infrastructure.

Meetings organised by the élite and calendared in national publications contrasted with the plebeian races held as a part of regular country festivities such as the Chapel Row[25] and Yattendon Revels,[26] or the Scouring of the White Horse.[27] Here farmers' hacks, cart-horses and ponies competed for a prize harness or bacon flitch within a programme of traditional contests of cheese-rolling, backswording, jingling and chase-the-pig. During the eighteenth century the gap between this robust, plebeian sport and that of the racecourse, where gentlemen competed on increasingly specialised horses, was widening. At the White Horse Scouring, for example, Lord Craven might fund the prizes and attend with his family as a paternalistic spectator, but he would not have dreamed of competing against his tenants cavorting across the downs on their assorted nags. A few weeks later those same tenants might gather to watch Lord Craven and his gentle friends race for a £50 plate at Lambourn, but the inferior quality of their horses and the race entry fees (not to mention possibly specific social criteria) would have excluded them from the starting line. The programme for Newbury/Woodhay Races of 1815 fell into two socially distinct halves: élite racing on the heath, followed the next week by plebeian sports on the town commons of Northcroft. Country racing's role in bridging these two social extremes of recreation was to become untenable as society polarised in the nineteenth century.

---

[25] HUMPHREYS. *Bucklebury*. p387
[26] BYNG. *Rides around Britain*. p67
[27] HUGHES. *Scouring of the White Horse*. p98-100

3

Runners and riders, rules and prizes
The conduct of racing on Georgian country courses

Pity the clerk. Whilst landowners provided land and cash, and the race committee laid down standards and procedures, it was the clerk of the course who undertook the detailed donkeywork of making race day happen.

He arranged dates, secured the venue, drummed up prize money, solicited entries, farmed out the multifarious concessions (which were often auctioned), liaised with local traders, laid out the course, organised the spectator facilities, stabling and scales, appointed the blacksmith, kept the accounts and publicised the event. He was usually a local lawyer, land agent or even the town clerk and, being of the middle classes, was plain Mr rather than an Esq. The post carried a salary, topped up by perhaps a cut of the race entry fees or, as at Reading and Newbury, a guinea from each winner.[1] When race day dawned he supervised everything except that which took place on the racetrack itself. The success of meetings depended heavily upon the efficiency of the clerk, and many made a profession of it, taking on more than one course. For most of the Newbury series in the early nineteenth century the clerk was an auctioneer called Richard Hiscock, a tenant of the Craven estate who lived at Stroud Green.

The stewards, in contrast, were unpaid and usually from the élite: JPs, MPs, landowners and military men. If not titled they would be labelled Esq. Their responsibility was to ensure fair play in the race, but that did not bar stewards from having runners themselves, nor from doubling up as starters and judges. It was piously presumed that no gentleman would take advantage of these responsibilities to advance his own racing interest.

Races in the early to mid-Georgian era were old-style matches, that is to say, based upon the one-to-one contest formula, although it became increasingly normal for three or four horses to take part. Each race was run in a series of four-mile heats until one horse had won twice. Half-an-hour between each heat allowed the horses to recover, and thus the day could be spun out with just one or two races. Even so, attracting runners was the

---

[1] BOYD. *Running horses.* p11

most arduous task of race organisation. Both spectators and clerks disliked walkovers, whereby one entry secured the prize without contest. Newbury in 1739 had only two runners for a £30 race, followed by a £10 walkover. In May 1740 Lambourn offered two races each day, with three runners in each. Abingdon in 1788 could muster only two races each with two runners, and a walkover, with the town purse of £50 attracting no runners at all. Reading did rather better in 1740, drawing sometimes up to six runners, but each race day still contained only one or two races.[2]

Chaotic starts could delay matters by an hour or more, either through inefficiency or because the starter had been bribed to create confusion, and thus unsettle a flighty favourite. The starting method varied from course to course. At Salisbury, where the start was out of sight, a musket shot told both horses and spectators that the race was under way, with further shots being discharged at the one, two and three mile posts.[3] Elsewhere a drumbeat was the signal, or the starter simply shouted 'Go!' (Flag starts were not introduced until early Victorian times.) Thereafter the pace was leisurely, with the first mile often taken at little more than walking pace. Indeed, at Winchester it was reported that the starter once overtook the entire field on his hack.[4] The finish was preceded by a distance post at 240 yards, and any horse which had not reached this point when the winner passed the finishing line was automatically disqualified from further heats.

Entrants were required to lodge their names and fees at a local inn a few days before the meeting. Late entrants paid a premium. At Ascot the advance fee was two guineas, or four at post. Reading in 1747 was one-and-a-half guineas, or three at post, to subscribers (those who had made a separate donation towards the race fund), or three/five guineas for those who had not. In 1712 Oxford's Port Meadow demanded from non-subscribers an additional guinea for every pound's worth of plate. There were also forfeits for entering and then withdrawing a horse from a race (a popular technique for manipulating the odds). Another boost for the race fund came from selling races, in which the winning horse was auctioned. Any surplus above a predetermined price would be split between the owner and the fund. Selling races were predominant in early Georgian race meetings — indeed a rule of 1712 at Oxford made all winners available for sale to race subscribers — but sellers tended to attract horses of the

---

[2] CHENY. *Historical list.* 1739, 1740 and *RC* 1788
[3] *VCH Wilts* vol iv p379-82
[4] FAIRFAX-BLAKEBOROUGH. *Analysis of the Turf.* p205

humbler variety, leading eventually to an association with lower quality meetings, and thus they declined in popularity.

Fig 9. Oxford Races in an engraving of 1799 by Sartorius. Three jockeys pass the distance post. Note the improbable posture of the horses. Not until the advent of cinematography was it realised that galloping horses do not extend all their legs simultaneously like this.

Some races had specific entry criteria. Reading's first calendared meeting in 1747 required that hunters could only be entered by residents of Berkshire or its neighbouring counties. Lambourn in 1801 ran a sweepstake for maidens which were owned by a freeholder of Berkshire. Banbury in 1831 limited one race to horses belonging to residents from within a 10-mile radius. Some races were restricted to a type of horse: hunters, galloways, ponies or even cart-horses.

The traditional prize of a major race of the seventeenth century was a bell, such as Salisbury's Golden Bell, returnable each year for the next winner. By early Georgian times the prize was generally a plate or cup, usually commuted into cash or a purse, although often still called a plate. Before 1740 country races ran for £10, £20 or £30 plates. After the Act £50 became the general standard, exceeded only by the King's Plates, which were worth £100. Introduced by Charles II and numbering 11 in 1721, these were increased to 15 by George II in 1752. They were bestowed upon racecourses thought to be making a positive contribution to national bloodstock. The only courses with royal plates within Newbury's hinterland were Ascot, Burford (until 1802), Salisbury and Winchester. Such races were the most prestigious and valuable in the national calendar for most of the eighteenth century, attracting famous horses. The Winchester royal plate of 1769 was won by the never-beaten *Eclipse*.

Some early prizes were funded outright by the local landowner, MP or the town council, but many were generated by subscription from supporters and tradesmen who benefited from race week. At Abingdon's meeting of 1807 the traditional Member's Purse hastily became the Steward's Purse because the newly elected MP, George Knapp, refused to pay up.[5] Several meetings ran Ladies' Plates, which were most certainly not for female riders, but were subscribed by a group of female race enthusiasts. Throughout the eighteenth century there was a drift towards sweepstake races, funded mostly from entry fees, with such added money as could be raised.

Winnings could be subject to a host of petty deductions, such as a guinea or two to the clerk of the course, or the cost of some champagne for race officials. At Port Meadow a positively punitive tariff greeted the winner: 20 shillings for flags and scales, three guineas to the clerk and 10 shillings for 'mending the course'. Often the judge would expect a gift, until the Jockey Club eventually outlawed such dubious practice. Ascot was liked by owners because it did not make such demands on winners.

One-to-one matches continued to be held, often as part of a race card also featuring races of multiple runners. Matches carried no prize money, but attracted monstrous wagers and generated high feeling. Grudges or personal animosity could ratchet up the stakes. The participants — invariably gentlemen or aristocrats — stood to gain or lose their reputation for judgment of horses, and this was no trivial matter. Reading advertised a 200-guinea match in 1776, on a race card of the more usual £50 prizes. Lord Abingdon's challenge to Lord Grosvenor at Newmarket in 1779 was worth 7,000 guineas. A rare and celebrated male-female contest was held at York in 1804 between one Mrs Alicia Thornton and a Mr Flint. The lady lost the match on day one, but won a rematch the next day. It was said that the crowd of 100,000 had £200,000 in wagers riding on the result. The Georgian world of racing also embraced single equestrian challenges, in which one owner-rider accepted a bet to complete some eccentric feat. Such a high-profile event took place at Newmarket in 1831, when George Osbaldeston,

---

[5] *JOJ* Sep 1807

a famous hunting squire who also raced in the Newbury area, accepted a wager to ride 200 miles in 10 hours on an unlimited number of horses. He completed the course in under nine hours, changing horses 50 times, and winning the bet of 1,000 guineas.[6] However such glitzy and gladiatorial events declined as racing became more professional. Matches represented 24 per cent of races in 1807, dwindling to seven per cent in 1843.[7]

Heat races exemplified the original rationale for racing — an heroic, manly activity with the patriotic purpose of improving cavalry horses — but the lumbering endurance test of 12 miles offered poor spectator sport. As the eighteenth century wore on race heats were gradually reduced in length and number. Royal plate rules reduced heats from four to three in 1773, by which time Jockey Club plates had abolished them altogether. Crowds wanted speed and uncertainty of outcome. Hence the trend was towards shorter races, bigger fields of more specialised, younger horses and professional (lightweight) jockeys. Three new races exemplified this trend; the St Leger (1776) at Doncaster, and the Oaks (1779) and the Derby (1780) at Epsom were dashes of a mile or so, created for three-year-olds, whose lack of established performance promised unpredictable results. These races were instant successes, followed at Newmarket in the early nineteenth century by the 2000 Guineas (1809) for colts and fillies, and the 1000 Guineas (1814) for fillies. During the first quarter of the nineteenth century these five races became known collectively as they are today: the Classics.

The word thoroughbred has been found in use as early as 1713,[8] but can have had little of its modern meaning then. In 1790 the Jockey Club instituted the General Stud Book under the pen of James Weatherby, from which point racehorse pedigrees were formally recorded, but this institution did not use the word thoroughbred until 1821.[9] Thereafter the term referred unambiguously to horses whose descent could be traced to one the three foundation sires imported in the early 1700s: the *Darley Arabian*, the *Godolphin Arabian* and the *Byerly Turk*.

A pseudonymous commentator from Hampshire in the mid-nineteenth century observed that 'horses running for King's Plates must have been very different from the wretched cat-legged creatures we now too frequently see start'.[10] Indeed they were. Carrying a rider of 12 stone or more

---

[6] WHYTE. *History of the British Turf.*
[7] EADIE. *Structure and organisation of English horseracing 1830-1860.*
[8] BARRETT. *Daily Telegraph chronicle of horse racing.*
[9] WHITE. *Racegoers' encyclopaedia.* p157
[10] AESOP. *Sporting reminiscence of Hampshire.* p25

for up to 12 miles, and standing typically at 14.1 hands, the racehorse of early Georgian matches was clearly a good deal sturdier than his descendants.[11] Even *Gimcrack* and *Flying Childers,* famous winners and sires of the early eighteenth century, were no more than 14.2 hands high, whereas the norm for a racehorse today is 15.2. Early racehorses carried a far higher proportion of eastern blood from the foundation sires, and they were characterised by strength, stamina and temperament that bore direct relevance to the requirements of the cavalry horse. As sprints or dashes replaced heat races, their descendants developed as larger but more delicate sprinters, bred for short and specialised careers.

Handicapping on the basis of past performance or estimated merit was unknown. It would in any case have worked directly against bloodstock improvement, which required that the best horse should always win. Whilst this philosophy prevailed weight allowances were granted only to take account of differing capability based on size or age. In early Georgian times give-and-take races allocated weight according to height, across the (then typical) range of 12 to 15 hands. As racehorses started their careers ever younger, give-and-take yielded to weight-for-age allowances. In the mid-eighteenth century horses were rarely in training before three years old, and most did not appear on the track until five, but by the later eighteenth century races for two- and three-year-olds were becoming popular. Size and age allowances were not true handicaps in that they did not equalise the field on the basis of form. The first public race based upon the modern idea of handicap was the Oatland Stakes at Ascot in 1790, which was an instant success, attracting vast wagers because it offered uncertainty of outcome. Thereafter handicap races spread, and were generally considered to be more prestigious than they are today. The Classics, however, remained true tests of merit.

The professional jockey was a product of the later eighteenth century. In earlier years the race rider would usually be the owner (hence the name of the Jockey Club). At Stockbridge in 1742 a three-heat sweepstake featured Fulke Greville, Lord Byron and the Earl of Berkeley riding their own horses.[12] Later in the century, Lord Barrymore was another regular owner-rider. In the event of an owner's incapacity, some likely lad from his stable might ride, in which case his name would be considered to be of no consequence, and would often be omitted from the record. But as races became faster and horses more specialised, the gentleman rider

---

[11] LAWRENCE. *History and delineation of the horse.*
[12] CHENY. *Historical list.* 1742

became a rustic anachronism, not to mention a liability. The riding standards of the hunting field were inappropriate for a valuable racehorse. By 1831 the *Sporting Magazine* could ridicule the sight of 'waving arms and yellow leather breeches in convulsions'. Nonetheless, such archaic and tubby heroes continued to gallop around the more traditional country courses. To compete with the lighter weighted professional jockeys, some portly gents resorted to drastic action. The fourth Lord Abingdon wrote of sweating off excess poundage by wearing seven waistcoats whilst buried in a dunghill.[13]

The rules of racing were rarely written down, most being a matter of local tradition. Royal plates were accompanied by a set of conditions published in 1744,[14] but these were not adopted for other races. Oxford was unusual in publishing its own set as early as 1712, wherein 17 regulations detailed weights, heats, flags and the means of resolution of disputes. The latter were to be decided by the gentleman-subscribers present, their probity in dispensing *ad hoc* judgment, even where they had an interest, being of course beyond question. In general however racecourse rules were mostly concerned with trade regulation (the sale of liquor near the racecourse was banned at Newbury) and entry conditions for particular races.

Little attempt was made to regulate conduct upon the track. Crossing and jostling was routine at country races, and jockeys made vigorous attempts to unseat each other. If one fell, any male spectator of the appropriate weight could mount the riderless horse and continue in his place. Another tradition permitted mounted spectators to join the runners in the closing furlongs of the race, often wreaking havoc with the result. The spectacle could be bloody, and fatalities were not unusual. In 1718 Sir Edward Longueville fell and broke his neck during a race at Bicester, just as his father had done in 1685. Horses which had the misfortune to be seriously injured were put down by having their throats cut. Most race advertisements threatened that all dogs found on the course would be destroyed, one four-legged species presumably being more than enough for thrills and spills. However an 1844 engraving of Reading Races depicts an apparently loose dog in the crowd, so perhaps this was not always enforced.

Robust practices on the track were matched by uncontrolled roguery prior to the race, often practised by those owners who also acted as stewards, starters and judges. The most respected aristocrats would routinely engineer false starts, or arrange for their horses to lose in order to

---

[13] ABINGDON. *Adieu to the Turf.*
[14] *RC* 1744

obtain better odds at a future race. (A losing jockey, however, risked being horsewhipped by disappointed backers.) Other forms of skullduggery included withdrawing horses at the last minute to leave long odds on others, and the substitution of a disguised, superior horse (a ringer, although the word was not used in this sense until 1890) for the one officially entered. Lord George Bentinck, successor to Bunbury as president of the Jockey Club and a noted reformer of racing, was not above painting his horse's nostrils with flour and water to give an appearance of ill-health, and, perhaps less reprehensibly, he fooled rivals with his 1836 St Leger entry, *Elis*, by keeping the horse in the south of England until a few days before the race. Odds lengthened, on the assumption of *Elis'* withdrawal from entry. At short notice Bentinck transported the horse by horse-drawn van (a startling innovation) to Doncaster in record time, having first of course secured favourably long odds on his wagers.

Doping had yet to be imported from the USA, but a bodged attempt at Newmarket in 1809 was a salutary example to any potential miscreant; two horses died after drinking from a trough laced with arsenic, and the perpetrator (but not those who had hired him) was hanged.[15] Nonetheless, a rival's horse might be covertly given a debilitating bucket of water just before the race. Alcohol was considered to be a stimulant, and many horses were given a draught of port or brandy before the off.

The Jockey Club was formed at Newmarket in 1752 as an association for wealthy racehorse owners. The word jockey at that time still meant owner, which was commonly synonymous with race rider. By 1758 its rules were formulated and published, and in 1762 racing colours were first registered, but the club carried no jurisdiction beyond Newmarket, nor did it seek to exert wider influence. No list of members was published until 1835, by which time there were around 80 — all aristocratic. Fulwar Craven the fourth baron had been one of the 19 founder members, and his three successors as Lord Craven were also members. The Jockey Club has been heavily criticised by sports historians for being primarily concerned with protecting its members' betting interests (which were also secured by their heavy representation in the House of Lords) rather than with raising the overall tone of the sport. Sporadically, the club was called in to arbitrate in local disputes, such as one raised by Charles Dundas at Lambourn races in 1790.[16] This intervention arose almost certainly through the agency of Lord

---

[15] *Horse racing: its history.* p366
[16] *RC* 1790

Craven, as a club member and Lambourn's landowner. It was more usual for country courses to cling fiercely to their own local traditions of authority. Not until the second quarter of the nineteenth century did the Jockey Club begin to introduce standards of conduct for race officials, but it had no statutory or economic power with which to enforce these sometimes costly reforms upon other courses.

Fig 10. The Jockey Club of 1790, by Thomas Rowlandson. The membership was known to have included: the Prince of Wales; the dukes of Bedford, Bolton, Devonshire, Grafton, Norfolk, Queensberry, St Albans and York; lords Barrymore, Clermont, Craven, Egremont, Foley, Grosvenor and Ossory; Sir Charles Bunbury and Sir John Lade; messrs. Fox, Panton, Vernon and Wastell. Of these, Bolton, Barrymore, Craven, Bunbury and Lade were regular patrons of racing in the Newbury area.

4

The Georgian racegoing experience
Comfort for spectators according to class

No turnstiles existed to count Georgian racegoers, but the figure of 8,000 has been estimated as typical for a 'small, socially inferior' meeting.[1] To compare with this we might consider the (possibly dubious) contemporary estimates of attendance at a few other one-off spectacles, comparing them with their modern-day equivalents. The Scouring of the White Horse in 1780 was claimed to have attracted a crowd of 30,000,[2] a remarkable turnout indeed for such a thinly populated area. Contrast this with the more accurately tallied 17,000 who attended the Hennnessy Cup at Newbury in 2004. The making of the Newbury Coat in 1811 (resulting from a wager between clothmaker John Coxeter and Sir John Throckmorton) was said to have been watched by 5,000, a figure which tallies neatly with Newbury's population in that year's census, but perhaps is not wholly unlikely given the inclusion of a free feast as part of the celebrations.[3] In 1818, according to a newspaper reader's letter, 7,000 spectators 'of all classes' watched the pedestrian feat of one Daniel Crisp, who walked 450 miles in six days around a marked course on Newbury's Wash Common.[4] Notwithstanding the allegedly massive White Horse throng, 4,000 - 8,000 seems a likely range of attendance for country race meetings in this area, although there would have been differences between the more remote downland locations and a well-connected urban centre such as Reading or Abingdon.

The spectator's means of transport defined his class. The vast majority of spectators came on foot, and 15 miles would not be an uncommon walking distance for a keen Georgian racegoer. Landowners, however, did not appreciate trespassers, even when bound for the races that they supported; in 1775 lords Harcourt and Nuneham forbade racegoers heading for Abingdon's Culham Heath to take a short cut through their private parkland.[5]

---

[1] HUGGINS. *Flat racing.* p119
[2] *RM* 15 May 1780
[3] ROBERTS. *And so to Bath.* p305-6
[4] *NWN* 18 May 1876
[5] *JOJ* 2 Sep 1775

However, public transport was constantly expanding during the eighteenth century, as more and more roads became turnpiked. Samuel Pepys recorded that the Bath-to-London coach got lost on the road between Newbury and Reading in 1668, and 30 years later Celia Fiennes found the same road to be 'sad clay deep way',[6] but by 1728 this route was turnpiked and humming with regular traffic. Cheapest was the covered stage-waggon which, led by the waggoner, trundled along at walking pace. The Oxford-to-Southampton service, calling in at Ilsley and Newbury, added Abingdon to its itinerary in 1772. Coaches drawn by four horses were faster, carrying up to six passengers inside at fourpence per mile, and up to 11 more clinging on outside at twopence. At seven to 10 miles per hour stage coaches could be both nauseous and dangerous, but Reading, Newbury and Abingdon were well-served with departures in all directions several times daily. The coaching trade was of particular importance to Newbury, because it was here that the majority of travellers to Bath – a fashionable crowd – stopped overnight, and a significant number planned their journeys to take in a prolonged stopover for the races, the Mansion House balls and the theatre.[7] Wantage and Faringdon lay on the coaching route west from Oxford to Swindon. East Ilsley, though small, straddled the busy north-south route that is now the A34. Only Lambourn, isolated deep in downland, struggled with poor transport links. It had a turnpike road of sorts by 1810, but as late as 1854 it had carrier connections only with Faringdon, Newbury, Marlborough and Wantage, and none of these daily.[8]

Smaller and more comfortable than the stage coach, and also operating a timetabled public service, was the diligence, which was drawn by two horses and carried four passengers. Price depended upon whether the vehicle had two wheels, or a superior foursome. Even more exclusive, a post-chaise driven by a postilion, and capable of around eight miles per hour, could be privately hired for between sixpence and one shilling per mile.[9] Families with any pretensions to gentility would have their own post-chaise, whilst carriages were, of course, the mark of the true gentry.

The river Kennet was navigable between Reading and Newbury by 1715, and in 1810 this was augmented by the opening of the Kennet and Avon Canal linking Reading with Hungerford and Bath. Passenger transport

---

[6] DILS. *Historical atlas of Berkshire.* p68
[7] PHILLIPS. *Great road to Bath.* p114-15
[8] *Billings directory* 1854
[9] ROSEVEAR. *Coach and waggon services across the upper Thames valley.* p7-13 and LA ROCHFOUCAULD. *Frenchman's year in Suffolk.* p5

was available in twice-weekly fly-boats (which had priority over the slower goods barges) in each direction. From 1810 the Wilts and Berks Canal linked the Thames at Abingdon with Wantage and Faringdon, eventually joining the Kennet and Avon Canal. Sadly, no specific account refers to racegoers using canal services, but Zacharias Conrad von Uffenbach, a visitor to Oxford's Port Meadow races in 1710, arrived by boat on the Thames, and noted several others doing so.[10]

Fig 11. The Oxford to Southampton stage waggon.

Road services depended upon a chain of reliable inns for fresh horses, victualling and accommodation on route. These same inns, numerous in the coaching towns of Abingdon, Hungerford, Newbury and Reading, were also heavily involved in race-week trade. Newbury's Castle, Cross Keys, Pelican, Globe and White Hart were typical hostelries which, as well as putting up travellers, acted as theatre box offices and entry registration points for the races. The Bath Road was used by everyone at some time or another. Daniel Defoe, William Hazlitt, Admiral Lord Nelson, Horace Walpole and the Duke of Wellington all passed through, and when the Earl of Chatham broke his journey to take up a prolonged convalescent

---

[10] CORDEAUX & MERRY. p57

residence in Marlborough's Castle Inn in 1767, it is tempting to wonder if the lure of the nearby races played any part in his decision to dally.[11]

No literary account of attending a local race meeting survives from this era, but a comparable occasion was the Great Fight at Hungerford in 1821 between two nationally famous pugilists, Bill Neate and Tom Hickman. William Hazlitt caught an early morning coach from London the day before, only to find that all accommodation in Newbury and Hungerford was already taken, such was the crush. He sat up all night in Newbury's Crown Inn before joining many thousands on Hungerford Common ('a rustic assembly - the cockneys distanced by 66 miles') to watch the fight. Neate won, and with £200,000 of wagers hanging on the result, the information was despatched to London by carrier pigeon.[12] The occasion must have had much in common with a busy race meeting.

Fig 12. A coaching supper at the Cross Keys Inn in Newbury, by George Cruikshank sen. The Cross Keys still stands, in London Road, although much altered since this period.

---

[11] PHILLIPS. *Great road to Bath.* passim
[12] HAZLITT. *Selected essays: the fight.* p83

There was no charge for entry to the race ground for those arriving on foot or on horseback, nor could there be on common land such as was used for Abingdon, Newbury, Reading, Marlborough and Oxford races. However, the view at ground level was often poor, as suggested by Abingdon's proud boast of 1767 that spectators would have an all-round view without moving from an 'easy eminence'.[13] Horseback improved visibility, and riders (invariably male) could enjoy social superiority above the rabble, as well as the freedom to move around the race ground swiftly and safely.

Carriages paid for the privilege of parking with a view of the course. This was the preference of those who wished to avoid rubbing shoulders with the masses. Parson Woodforde took five ladies to Bruton races in Norfolk in 1795, having hired a coach in which the party spent the entire afternoon incarcerated at great discomfort in the summer's heat.[14] However most courses had grandstands by 1800, where the middle classes, and ladies in particular, could buy comfortable seclusion from the noisome masses. These were run as separate, subscription-based enterprises, and entry was by no means cheap. The five-shilling charge for a gentleman equated very nearly to a labourer's weekly wage. A gateman (often a former pugilist) would be employed to keep riff-raff out. We know of a grandstand at Newbury in 1812, thanks to the survival of a badge in the British Museum, and records exist of Abingdon's grandstand, built by the corporation in 1812 and leased to the racing committee. Some grandstands were temporary, and shoddily built; a Port Meadow scaffold collapsed in 1733, killing several spectators. Thomas Hearne noted that it had been erected by a local carpenter with a record for poor workmanship.[15] Permanent (and presumably more sturdy) grandstands were often used for other public entertainments such as cricket matches or prizefights, and are sometimes the last surviving evidence of a former racecourse, either on the ground or marked on a map. The grandstand at Stockbridge, last used in 1898, stood until very recently as an ivy-clad ruin on private land.

Provided that the grandstand did not collapse it was a desirable option, given the lack of crowd control. In the absence of rails spectators frequently surged onto the course, and safety was a continual problem for the organisers. A horse was injured at Port Meadow in 1710 by a woman running on to the course. The newspaper account does not record whether

---

[13] *News of a country town.* 1767
[14] WOODFORDE. *Diary of a country parson.* p229
[15] CORDEAUX & MERRY. p60-1

she suffered the same fate as a dandy who got in the way of the 1818 Derby, for which he was horsewhipped off the downs. Horses were brought down by wandering spectators at Ascot in 1752,[16] and at Banbury in 1831.[17] After remodelling in 1774, Reading racecourse advertised 'a safe and convenient place for those on foot to see the sport, and some will be permitted to come onto the ground betwixt the distance and winning posts, and it is hoped that none will attempt...'[18] Sadly, the newsprint becomes illegible at this point, so the precise folly must be imagined. At Enborne in 1805 the advertisement expressed the pious hope that spectators would 'retire behind the cords' while the race was running, but clearly there was no practical means of ensuring this.[19] Abingdon's meeting of 1817 was congratulated for having not a single accident – apparently a remarkable occurrence.[20] This problem endured well into the Victorian era, when Oxford solved its difficulties by employing a huntsman and four whips from the Heythrop to patrol along the cords.[21]

Good weather contributed significantly to the pleasure of racegoing, but cancellation was impractical without modern communications, and the general public had to endure whatever the heavens bestowed upon them. Jane Austen's letters lament two days of wretched weather at Basingstoke Races in 1813, and her last work, dictated on her death-bed in 1817, was a satirical poem about Winchester Races, which were apparently renowned for wet weather.[22] It can scarcely have been worse than Abingdon in 1828, when the fashionable ladies were drenched, and horses were alleged to have been running up to their knees in water.[23] Bad weather was, of course, equally bad for trade, and after an inclement meeting in 1767 the Duke of Marlborough distributed more than 20 guineas to Port Meadow stallholders to compensate for their reduced takings.[24]

An abundance of ancillary entertainments accompanied the races, both on and off the race ground. Pitches and booths on course were rented out to sellers of beer and food, shooting galleries, bands, organ-grinders,

---

[16] MAGEE. *Ascot.* p27
[17] BROWN-GRANT. p73
[18] *RM* 21 Aug 1775
[19] *RM* 19 Aug 1805
[20] *JOJ* 20 Aug 1817
[21] CORDEAUX & MERRY. p62
[22] SELWYN. *Poetry of Jane Austen.* p17-18
[23] JOJ 13 Sep 1828
[24] CORDEAUX & MERRY. p61

Fig 13. An Extensive View of the Oxford Races, by Charles Turner (1773-1857) also shown in colour on the front cover. The picture is undated, but the costume suggests early nineteenth century, and is a rare depiction of a country racecourse in that it shows the crowd rather than an actual race. The grandstand on the right is labelled 'Appelby's Stand'. This has a staircase, unlike the more rickety-looking stand in the far distance, accessed via a steep ladder. Drinks are being served from the bottom right-hand corner of the picture; a figure carrying a tray of bottles and glasses crosses in front of a small boy carrying a boiling kettle. Women are well represented in the crowd, and there is a significant military presence.

fire-eaters, rope-dancers, acrobats, performing dogs and Gypsy fortune-tellers. The longueurs between heats could be easily filled with these diversions. A typical booth rental might be one guinea, but those likely to make the greatest gains were also expected to give a donation towards the race prizes. Victualling concessions on the racecourse were usually protected for local traders, and at Abingdon, Ascot and Burderop there was a requirement for racehorses to be stabled and shod ahead of the races at a subscribing local farrier.

Foremost among the beneficiaries of race week were local inns, which acted as multi-purpose booking offices, transport termini, livery stables, contact points, delivery depots and even hairdressing salons. The sale of liquor during race week was heavily protected, and a posse raised by Abingdon to stop beer sales on the Lord's Day in 1812 was really more concerned with the fact that some booths had been erected by 'divers persons from another parish in another county'.[25] Lambourn too forbade liquor sales by any other than publicans of the parish who had paid at least one guinea into the race fund of 1785. Not for nothing were country race meetings dubbed 'publicans' races'.[26]

The inns served ordinaries, which were special race-week *table d'hôte* meals for the middling class of racegoer. Usually these were for men only, or sometimes separate male and female sessions would be scheduled. The Star Inn of Oxford broke new ground in 1829 by introducing mixed tables. Advertisements indicate that a co-operative system allocated ordinaries to a different inn for each race day.[27] The Newbury ordinaries of 1805 were shared between the George & Pelican, and the Globe. In 1810 the menu was supplemented by a gracious donation of venison from Lord Craven's deer park. Reading's ordinaries of 1747 rotated between the Upper Ship, the Black Bear and the New Inn, with the admonition that the meal would be served at exactly two pm each day. Racing, scheduled to start at four, was clearly not to be delayed by dilatory diners.

Sophisticated and specialised services might have to be imported for race week. Ladies of fashion could not be expected to attend the race ball or theatre uncoiffed. London hairdressers and perfumiers advertised their presence in Abingdon for the race weeks of 1775 and 1781,[28] and at

---

[25] *JOJ* 15 Jul 1812
[26] *Baily's turf guide.* (1860) p86
[27] *JOJ* 19 Sep 1767
[28] *JOJ* 16 Sep 1775 & 6 Oct 1781

Winchester in 1788.[29] They too based themselves in local inns for the duration. But inns did not have a total monopoly of the accommodation market; the influx of visitors to two- and three-day meetings, topped and tailed by social events, could even warrant the temporary vacation of family homes for profitable letting.[30] During Abingdon's race week of 1769 a Mrs Harness advertised that she had hired a 'large, commodious house' for the purposes of renting out rooms.[31]

Cockfighting and prizefighting usually took place during race week, either on the racecourse or at nearby inns, many of which had their own pits, either indoor or outdoor. Cockfighting was a gentleman's sport, but it was popular across the social spectrum until the 1820s, by which time it was becoming disreputable, although the tradition hung on for some decades in Newbury. Newspaper advertisements for mains (as cocking bouts were called) were undersigned by feed suppliers such as Bromley and Coxhead at Reading in 1774, and Eaton and Bromley at Abingdon in 1776,[32] suggesting early instances of commercial sponsorship.

Prizefighting was technically illegal from 1750, but the ban was widely ignored. On the day after Abingdon Races finished in 1809, thousands gathered on Culham Heath to watch a 50-round prizefight which lasted for nearly two hours. Prizefighting traditionally enjoyed the patronage of the aristocracy in Georgian times, although this waned as fight-fixing increased, and magistrates began to exert their authority.

Race-week balls were held in the local assembly rooms or town hall, and the ticket price of five shillings for ladies and seven-and-sixpence for gentlemen suggests that they were aimed upmarket, at the grandstand clientèle. Newbury's 300 guests at the Mansion House in 1805 were described as being 'of the first fashion and distinction',[33] and indeed a well-attended ball could go some way towards ameliorating a poor racing turnout. The occasion might be used to obtain subscriptions for the following year's meeting. Reading race ball of 1777 was the subject of an anonymous poem eulogising the beauty of the high-society ladies who attended. Indeed, though entitled Reading Races, the poem makes no

---

[29] AESOP. *Sporting reminiscences of Hampshire.* p25
[30] HUGGINS. *Flat racing.* p145
[31] *JOJ* 16 Sep 1769
[32] *JOJ* 7 Sep 1776
[33] *RM* 19 Aug 1805

reference to them, as though the ball itself were the defining event of race week.[34]

More substantial towns had theatres running special race-week programmes, with London casts and a different play each night. Here all classes attended, albeit segregated by seat price. At Newbury's Pelican Theatre quality folk paid three shillings apiece for a box seat, whilst lesser spectators occupied the pit at two shillings or the gallery at one. During the race week of 1807 they could see William Henry West Betty, a juvenile lead of national fame, play Richard III among an adult cast, although light comedies were more usual. Reading Theatre in 1799 advertised a race-week production entitled *Laugh When You Can,* performed by His Majesty's Servants from the Theatre Royal, Windsor. Henry Thornton's company toured the race-town theatres regularly (Newbury, Oxford, Abingdon, Marlborough and Reading) with a cast that included Dorothy Jordan, former mistress of the future William IV; his repudiation of her had obliged her to return to the stage. A more select, invited audience would have attended the private theatres of the Margravine of Anspach (formerly Lady Craven) at Benham Valence, and Lord Barrymore at Wargrave.[35] However the margravine was also a supporter of the Pelican, and sometimes brought her own productions to the town centre assembly rooms in Newbury.

Violent disturbances were unusual at racecourses, but crime was rife in the spectator area. Pickpockets and prostitutes were regular racegoers, and clerks cheerfully rented pitches to assorted fraudsters such as thimble-riggers[36] and card-sharps, whose sole intent was to take cash off naïve spectators by a variety of confidence tricks.[37] If caught in the act, pickpockets and other assorted cheats could expect little mercy from the crowd. Beatings were commonplace, as was ducking in the nearest pond or river, and sometimes ears were cropped to make the miscreant easily recognisable at future meetings. One such crook was killed at Ascot in 1791, and the Duke of Cumberland is credited with the rescue of another at Epsom in 1773.[38] Following an incident at Reading in 1814 two pickpockets were severely

---

[34] *Reading races.* (1777)

[35] RANGER. *Catalogue of strolling companies: ongoing theatre in Newbury.* p13-14

[36] Thimble-rigging was a version of the three-card trick, using three thimbles and a pea.

[37] VAMPLEW. *Turf.* p139

[38] *Horse racing: its history and early records of the principal and other race meetings.* p303-4

ducked in the Thames,[39] and Banbury's eventful 1831 meeting included the ducking of a pickpocket in the Cherwell. The majority, however, presumably escaped with easy pickings.

But whatever the hazards for spectators, it would appear that Georgian racegoing was seen as a wholesome family outing. Zacharias Conrad von Uffenbach, visiting Oxford in 1710, fumed when he found the Ashmolean Library closed because the sub-librarian had gone to the races at Port Meadow.[40] A county court clerk of Abingdon confessed that he 'did go away to Abingdon Races and leave the said jury confined some space of times' in 1782.[41] Jane Austen attended Newbury and Basingstoke races, and made several other references to racegoing in her letters.[42] Caroline Lybbe Powys recorded visits to Maidenhead and Reading races with her mother in the 1780s.[43] People from all walks of life, and their children attended, probably as much for the opportunity of reunion with friends and family as for watching the sport. Even men of the cloth could go without fear of censure, and many described such visits in their diaries; Parson Woodforde, though not of this area, noted several and, more locally, the Rev. George Woodward of East Hendred, broke his coach journey to London to attend Maidenhead Races in 1760.[44] The following year the Rev. James Newton of Nuneham Courtenay recorded a visit to Port Meadow.[45]

---

[39] BOYD. *Running horses.* p11

[40] CORDEAUX & MERRY. p57

[41] BOYD. *Running horses.* p12

[42] CHAPMAN. *Jane Austen's letters.* p204, 205, 235, 342-43

[43] POWYS. *Passages from the diaries of Mrs Philip Lybbe Powys 1756-1808.* p226

[44] WOODWARD. *Parson in the Vale of the White Horse: letters from East Hendred 1753-1761* Sep/Oct 1760

[45] NEWTON. *Deserted village: diary of an Oxfordshire rector 1736-86.* 20 Aug 1761

5

'All the impudence of emboldened profligacy'
Georgian gamblers and general disapproval of racing

The Georgian age was characterised by prodigious gambling by the upper classes on horse races, cards, cockfights, boxing, billiards, pedestrian feats and indeed almost any event of uncertain outcome. The Prince of Wales might turn to Parliament to make good his debts, but family fortunes more commonly took the brunt. The euphoria of notoriety – seemingly almost an incentive to excess – soon withered into the unendurable disgrace of bankruptcy. Some might flee the country; others chose what was considered to be the gentleman's way out. The Derbys of 1813 and 1836 were both credited with the suicide of ruined gamblers, the latter victim being the sixth Lord Craven's younger son Augustus Berkeley Craven (1777 - 1836). His £8,000 losses in backing the field against the winner *Bay Middleton* led him to shoot himself the morning after the race. Nor was gambling confined to men; Lord Abingdon's poem makes passing reference to creditors circling Lady Bampfylde, a racehorse owner and prominent patron of Stockbridge and Reading.[1] Almost all owners bet in order to fund their racing interest, because prize money was negligible in relation to the costs of ownership, and there were as yet no significant returns to be had from the bloodstock market.

Gentlemanly wagers were initially conducted on a credit basis, one-to-one, off-course. In response to the evident demand for some fixed premises for these deals, Richard Tattersall, a horse auctioneer, set up rooms at Hyde Park Corner in 1815. The entry requirements for Tattersalls were socially stringent, demanding good breeding as well as sound funding. At a lower social level wealthy farmers were beginning to aspire to gentrified lifestyles, including field sports and gambling and, whilst not in the four- and five-figure league of the aristocratic gamblers, they thought nothing of losing £40 a day at the races.[2] La Rochefoucauld, observing English racing for the first time in 1784, noted that racing wagers were unwritten, and that they

---

[1] ABINGDON. *Adieu to the Turf.*
[2] MINGAY. *English landed society in the eighteenth century.* p249

were settled the day after the races at local coffee houses.[3] Such were the protocols of gambling amongst gentlemen (both actual and aspirational), whose word was their bond.

Changes were afoot by 1800. Shorter, faster races with younger horses, and handicap races based upon form were an instant success with racegoers, and they pushed a growing interest in betting further down the social scale. Tattersalls and credit were not relevant here. Betting stands and posts became a feature of even modest courses such as Enborne during 1805 - 1811, suggesting that a significantly public level of cash betting was now taking place on the course.

The prototype bookmakers were called blacklegs. These betting entrepreneurs came from lowly origins, and were despised by the upper classes who first used them. Indeed, the name expressed patrician scorn for their plebeian dress – blacklegs wore top boots because they could not afford stockings. The *Oxford English Dictionary* dates this usage of 'blackleg' from 1771 (defining it as 'turf swindler'), and the fourth Earl of Abingdon used the phrase in his poem of 1778, *Adieu to the Turf*

> *to see Dukes Jockies Blacklegs join'd*
> *...fly thru thick clouds of dust and sweat*
> *All jostle alltogether*

The relationship between blacklegs and their aristocratic customers was uneasy, as suggested by the lines above. That upper and lower classes should mingle in circumstances without the clear subordination of the latter to the former was novel, and disturbing to some.

Blacklegs did not bet in the round, that is to say they did not make a balanced book on all the runners but simply offered odds on one or two horses. A win by a local favourite could place them in a precarious position, and the blackleg might occasionally slip away without honouring his obligations. At the conclusion of Abingdon Races in 1768 it was observed that 'some of the lower classes [were] said to have decamped without making their Appearance after the Treats; from whence it is shrewdly conjectured that some trifling punctilios were not properly adjusted'.[4] This oblique statement is open to several possible interpretations, but the most likely is that one or two blacklegs had made off without settling their

---

[3] LA ROCHEFOUCAULD. *Frenchman's year in Suffolk.*
[4] *JOJ* 1 Oct 1786

bargains. Gambling debts were not recoverable at law, a situation which offered an incentive to dishonesty but, Abingdon Races notwithstanding, most social historians are of the opinion that blacklegs were usually men of their word.

The legal status of gambling was confused. Legislation of 1710 decreed that a punter losing a stake of more than £10 could take legal action to recover his money. In the same year it was made illegal to bet more than £10. Unsurprisingly, the former law was rarely invoked, and the latter was largely ignored by the authorities.[5]

Social historians have frequently asserted that before the mid-nineteenth century gambling on horses was of no interest to ordinary people, being beyond their pockets. The idea is hard to sustain. People were familiar with EO tables (a precursor of roulette), cards and games such as pitch-and-toss played for money. Racecourses abounded with gambling sideshows, indicating the readiness of ordinary spectators to chance their money. Cockfighting's *raison d'être* was gambling. The 1740 Act, in weeding out low-grade race meetings, sought specifically not only to protect the quality of bloodstock, but also to lessen 'the impoverishment of the meaner sort'. This is a clear indication that betting on horses tempted those on low incomes, and to a degree that worried the ruling class. This fear is borne out by La Rochefoucauld's observation in 1784 of 'a great number of people who economise all through the year for the pleasure of risking the product of the year's privation on one five-minute fling'.[6]

This was the age of national lotteries, until their abolition in 1826. There were also private lotteries; Abingdon Races ran raffles during race week, although a labourer would scarcely have been able to find the ticket price of one or two guineas. The prize in 1767 was a new four-wheeled post-chaise, and in 1782 a 'high-bred bay mare'.[7] Sweepstake betting (as distinct from sweepstake races) was introduced in 1750, and fell at first into a similar category with stakes priced at £1, but it was later targeted at lighter pockets with stakes of more like sixpence or a shilling. As might have been predicted, publicans were usually behind raffles and sweepstakes.

If Georgian racing acknowledged any principle, it was that horses should always be run on their merits – making every effort to win – but the primacy of owner interest was another powerful and sometimes conflicting ethic. Owners were assumed to have the right to operate in their own best

---

[5] VAMPLEW. *Turf.* p200
[6] LA ROCHEFOUCAULD. *Frenchman's year in Suffolk.* p46
[7] *JOJ* 19 Sep 1767 and 21 Sep 1782

interests, without regard to other people's money on the race. Hence horses were frequently entered for races in which they were never intended to run; whatever forfeit was incurred by withdrawal might be more than offset by the gains made through odds on other horses. Bets of this era were 'play-or-pay', which meant that stakes were not returnable in the event of the horse not running. Odds were often quoted on owners rather than on the horse itself, but curiously, in the light of this, disguising an owner was not considered to be gross malpractice, whereas disguising the horse most certainly was. Successful owners often entered under false names, sometimes for reasons of social discretion, but more often to keep long odds on their horses. Inside knowledge, therefore, was of immense importance for successful betting.

In the absence of mass communications race results trickled out by word of mouth, mail-coach drivers being key transmitters. For big races and other major sporting events pigeons or even trail-trained hounds might be used to carry the news. Such primitive methods could have been superseded by the electric telegraph, invented in the 1830s, but this was only slowly adopted by racecourses. Stockbridge was not connected until 1870. Within such uncertainty on timing and information it was by no means impossible for off-course wagers to be made with one party (it could be either) already enjoying private knowledge of the result.

Race meetings attracted other forms of gambling, some of which the organisers could control. EO tables were banned from the town of Newbury, presumably with the co-operation of the municipal authority, during the race weeks of 1805 - 1815, to channel gambling expenditure onto the racecourse, where operators had paid for their presence. Oxford too attempted to suppress gambling sideshows in 1828.[8] The authorities could not, however, regulate private wagering scenarios arranged by the gambling fraternity. Billiards matches, and a host of scams associated with them, followed the racing calendar. Andrew Steinmetz described an elaborate sting set up in 1794 around an unwitting star player from Windsor. The first match took place at Epsom Races, the next at Ascot, and thence, it was intended, to a profitable culmination at Winchester Races. The scheme fell apart when the outraged player refused to throw the third game.[9]

The association of racing with sin engaged the clergy and the godly laity. As a racegoer Jane Austen probably wrote with tongue in cheek when

---

[8] CORDEAUX & MERRY. p63
[9] STEINMETZ. *Gaming table, its votaries and victims.* vol 2 ch vii

she confected her poetic tale of Winchester races and St Swithin, the city's patron saint. The townsfolk, she claimed, had failed to ask his permission before organising 'these races and revels and dissolute measures' and the response of the saint (long associated with the prediction of summer rain) was to place a curse upon Winchester's race week.

> *Ye cannot but know my command o'er July*
> *Henceforward I'll triumph in shewing my powers*
> *Shift your race as you will it will never be dry*
> *The curse upon Venta[10] is July in showers—*[11]

More seriously, an anti-racing campaign in Cheltenham was led by the Rev. Francis Close, who published a virulent condemnation of racing in 1827. He lambasted racecourses as places where

> *prostitution, licentiousness forsake the lurking place...and stalk abroad in all the impudence of emboldened profligacy.* [12]

His followers disrupted Cheltenham's meetings and burned down the grandstand, causing the races to be relocated briefly to Tewkesbury. Flat racing returned to Cheltenham's Prestbury Park in 1831, but the fervent cleric (now promoted to dean) and an unsympathetic landowner combined to suppress these meetings by the 1840s.[13]

Oxford University was always an enemy of Port Meadow's meetings. A seventeenth-century letter remarks that a number of undergraduates who went to the races were punished with impositions on their return to college. A statute of 1772 forbade any engagement of members in racing on pain of rustication.[14] However the 1828 attempt to suppress on-course gambling at Port Meadow would have made little effect upon undergraduates who, as members of the upper class, would normally have made their wagers off-course on the basis of credit.

---

[10] *Venta Belgarum* was the Roman name for Winchester.
[11] SELWYN. *Poetry of Jane Austen.* p17-18
[12] CLOSE. *Evil consequences of attending the racecourse exposed in a sermon.*
[13] HUGGINS. *Flat racing.* p207
[14] CORDEAUX & MERRY. p56, 62

Opposition to racing on grounds of animal welfare was in its infancy in Georgian times, although the world of sporting gentlemen was not entirely insensate to animal suffering. The *Gentleman's Magazine* protested against cruelty in racing, the excessive use of whip and spur and the general treatment of racehorses which, it claimed, was worse than that of hackneys. Of a 40-hour London-to-York match run in 1773 the magazine expostulated that there was 'no name disgraceful enough to characterise this sort of diversion'.[15] Another commentator fulminated against the brutality of race riding in 1809, noting that unsuccessful racehorses were sold into gruelling draught work to which they were unsuited.[16]

The *Sporting Magazine* also was unusually outspoken against the ill-treatment of horses, on the racetrack and in horse feats, which spanned a variety of bizarre endurance tests. In 1799 it roundly denounced 'Counsellor Lade', a recently deceased misanthrope, and lately resident at Cannon Park, a large but reportedly inhospitable mansion at Kingsclere, a few miles south of Newbury. (The house was demolished, but later the renowned Park House yard of John Porter was built nearby.) Possibly he was a relative of Sir John Lade, the Prince of Wales' friend, who also lived and kept racehorses at the same establishment a few years later. The counsellor, according to the magazine, raced regularly around a circuit that included Epsom, Ascot, Egham, Reading, Oxford, Abingdon and Lambourn.[17] The obituary fulminated against Lade's harsh treatment of not only his racehorses but also his brood mares and carriage horses. All were overworked and underfed because of Lade's parsimony, to such an extent that the racehorses, some of which were highly bred, usually performed badly on the track. When taken away for sale after Lade's death, the sorry procession of emaciated beasts apparently excited universal pity in the towns and villages through which they passed. The magazine spared no effort in its condemnation of this behaviour in a diatribe spanning two successive issues of the magazine.

The Society for Prevention of Cruelty to Animals (SPCA) was founded in 1824. An early president was the third Earl of Carnarvon, son of the second earl who had supported Newbury Races in the early nineteenth century. The early SPCA tended to concentrate on working animals,

---

[15] *Gentleman's Magazine* vol 28 (1758), vol 26 (1756) p417-18, vol 43 (1773) p410
[16] LAWRENCE. *History and delineation of the horse.*
[17] *Sporting Magazine* Dec 1799 and Jan 1800

although the more brutal blood sports of the working man were temptingly soft targets for the reformers. Bull-baiting (whereby dogs attacked a tethered bull, supposedly to tenderise its meat) was very popular in Newbury and Wantage. Cock-throwing, another Newbury favourite, involved sticks being thrown at a tethered cockerel until it could no longer stand. Such animal-baiting was outlawed in 1835, as was cockfighting in 1845.[18] Racing tended to incite more mixed feelings amongst the middle classes; some saw the meetings as licensed bacchanalia, whilst in other areas racing was seen as a relatively civilised alternative to the more savage sports of the lower orders. Bucklebury's pony-racing was promoted as a more wholesome recreation than the blood-soaked backswording bouts of the Chapel Row Revels in the 1830s.

In 1843 the SPCA instituted a rare prosecution in Newbury concerning horse racing, albeit of an old-fashioned variety. In the course of a two-horse race from Bath to Newbury, the defendant was found guilty of cruelty and torture of his horse (which he drove to death along the Bath Road). *The Times* lamented the inadequacy of the £5 fine, expressing the view that imprisonment with hard labour would have been more appropriate.[19] Significantly, the defendant was a tavern-keeper, not a scion of Berkshire's aristocracy.

Patrician pleasures such as fox-hunting, shooting, coursing and thoroughbred racing enjoyed a degree of immunity from the middle-class reformers, whose mission was to improve the moral calibre of the working man, not to antagonise the ruling class. Flat racing thus escaped criticism, except when it came under the scrutiny of tender-hearted foreigners; Zacharias Conrad von Uffenbach found two days' racing at Port Meadow in 1710 to be quite enough 'unless you are an Englishman, fond of torturing horses, and take pleasure in overdoing the poor animals'.[20]

He would have been even more appalled by steeplechasing, which is covered in the next chapter.

---

[18] GOLBY & PURDUE. p78
[19] *The Times* 2 Jan 1843
[20] CORDEAUX & MERRY. p57

6

Over the jumps
Hunting, steeplechasing, hurdling and point-to-point

In the popular imagination there is a timeless image of fox-hunters taking formidable natural obstacles in their galloping stride. In fact this scene belongs mainly to the era since 1750. Until then English hunting quarry was mostly deer or hare, involving a relatively leisurely chase. The riders usually dismounted to negotiate obstacles, and a contributory factor to moderating the pace was probably the need for most of the horses to be fit for work the next day.

Foxes (the hunting of which increased as stags became less numerous) ran faster and more deviously, speeding up the chase. Additionally, the countryside was increasingly subject to enclosure, albeit with wide variations according to terrain. Newbury and its environs split between the boggy clay of the Kennet Valley, heavy hunting country which was relatively slow to be enclosed, and the better drained chalk turf of the Berkshire and Hampshire downs, land of higher farming quality and more suited to the chase. Here as in so many other parts of the country, hunting evolved into a faster pursuit over jumps. Both hounds and horses began to be bred for a different and more specialised purpose. Thus the evolution of English hunters into racehorses (by the addition of eastern blood) acquired an obverse; by 1800 the ideal hunter was itself half-racehorse.

Hunt territories were relatively amorphous in the early days, depending upon the land-holding of the hunt owner and his local alliances. William and Fulwar Craven, brothers and third and fourth barons respectively, created one of the earliest packs of fox-hounds in 1739. One local tradition locates Fulwar Craven's kennels at Hamstead Marshall, but it is more certain that he kept a pack at Ashdown, closer to the heart of better fox-hunting country. Here he was commemorated in the picture *The Kill at Ashdown,* painted by James Seymour, a work renowned as the first to depict fox-hunting. The Craven Hunt continued to be maintained by his next three successors, each of whom served as masters.[1] Lord Abingdon too created a hunt named after himself, based at Rycote. Individual hunts prospered

---

[1] CRAVEN. unpublished family memoir.

directly according to the influence of their owners, quite a few of whom were wealthy enough to maintain more than one kennels; Lord Craven also kept hounds at Dummer, in Hampshire. No subscriptions were involved, and these hunts were run as private fiefs. Access to tenanted land was taken for granted by landlords, although this was sometimes resented by farmers. Amalgamations of territory and transfers of hounds took place regularly between hunts, as did some acrimonious disputes about turf.

By 1800 hunts were linked to racing, with many meetings scheduling a hunt race or two. This was logical, given the overlap of patronage between the two activities. Hunt masters might sponsor a race for their participants to give them a training focus outside the hunting season. They might equally sponsor a race for obliging farmers, such as the one held on Tichborne Down by the Hambledon Hunt in 1794. The Mostyn Hunt organised a similar meeting in Oxfordshire in 1809, restricted to gentlemen. In keeping with the early character of hunting, these races were on the Flat.

Steeplechasing evolved from the hunt tradition, but relatively slowly, and separately. Most racing histories locate the first steeplechase in County Cork in 1752, although 'pounding matches', as they were then called, had probably existed for some time before. The *Oxford English Dictionary* dates the word steeplechase from 1793, although the *Victoria County History* for Hampshire claims a startling early example for Winchester.[2] Here a 'steeplechase' was supposedly held in 1788, although it was more likely to have been an early hunt race on the Flat.

English steeplechases began as one-to-one cross-country contests like the Irish pounding matches, but from 1800 they began to evolve into public races with larger fields. The first military steeplechase took place in 1804. The link was natural; Flat racing, with its increasingly specialised horses and professional jockeys no longer offered cavalry officers the opportunity to test their manly skills and mounts in a context of endurance riding. The end of the French wars in 1815 swelled the numbers of returning officers, who sought to hone their horsemanship in competition. Military steeplechase meetings became regular events.

The first purpose-built steeplechasing course was constructed at Bedford for a meeting in 1810. Entrants (who qualified via hunt participation) faced eight fences, each four-foot-six high, and with a heavy top bar. As with old-style Flat races, they competed in heats. Forty-thousand spectators were claimed for this event, although cross-country courses presented obvious problems of visibility for spectators. Even the officials

---

[2] *VCH Hants* vol v p545 quoting AESOP. *Sporting reminiscences of Hampshire.*

had to stand on farm waggons to view the finish. In 1830 the first steeplechase course in the round was constructed at St Albans, and staged with the manifest intention of attracting a crowd. Unfortunately, the exemplary standard of provision for spectators could not avoid a tragic outcome on the track; the winning horse, *Grimaldi,* dropped dead just beyond the post.

The sport acknowledged no rules or precedents, and was in a sense a return to the more robust forms of early Georgian racing, mixed with elements of hunting: big fields of heavier, cross-bred horses; open country courses of four miles or more; some formidable obstacles; little provision for spectators or gambling. Moreover, the riders were mostly amateur. Such was the stamina of these early steeplechasers, it was apparently normal in Buckinghamshire to race at 11am and go stag-hunting at noon, with an outward and homeward journey of perhaps 20 miles to boot.[3]

Steeplechasing appealed to students at Oxford University, perhaps because it circumvented the ban on their participation in Flat racing. Their early fixtures tended to be long-distance, one-to-one matches. In 1818 two undergraduates undertook a punishing 25-mile course from Chinery Court to Nettlebed in Oxfordshire, and two years later another pair raced from Hartford Bridge to Mortimer in Hampshire. Unable to traverse the Duke of Wellington's estate at Stratfield Saye, they took different directions around it, and did not meet for an hour.[4] College authorities moved to suppress such activities, but the undergraduates found a powerful ally in the professor of political economy, who was an avid fan. By 1848 there was an Oxford University Steeplechase established at Banbury, specifically for undergraduates.[5]

Perhaps unsurprisingly, steeplechasing never achieved the social cachet of Flat racing. The winter season was less attractive to fashionable attendance, prize money was lower and the economic potential for bloodstock distinctly limited where the runners were usually geldings. The equine attrition rate was punishing to a degree that deterred the owners of valuable thoroughbreds. Critics were particularly concerned that heroic horses would give their all, without the benefit of brief pauses to regain wind, such as were afforded in the hunting field. The example of *Grimaldi* seemed to vindicate such criticism. Small wonder that the patricians of the Jockey Club condemned steeplechasing as a 'bastard amusement which no true sportsman who values his horse would countenance'. Nonetheless, the

---

[3] FOWLER. *Echoes of old country life.* p93
[4] SETH-SMITH. *History of steeplechasing.*
[5] FOWLER. *Echoes of old country life.* p6, 168

sport spread rapidly across England, and some Flat enthusiasts participated, albeit not with their Flat horses. At least three members of the Craven family maintained interests in both sports simultaneously.

Following St Albans there was an explosion of country steeplechases in the late 1830s, some on prepared courses, but many still over open farmland. Eleven runners went to post at Tetworth, Oxon, in 1832, and a steeplechase was also held at Bicester in this decade. Heats, which limited the number of fences, soon gave way to larger fields in a single four-mile dash over many more fences. A few standard practices emerged, but it would be premature to talk of rules in a sport which was characterised chiefly by wild riding. Entries qualified through local hunting experience, horses being required to have been in at three kills, but this could be circumvented either by renting a property judiciously sited on the boundary of two or three hunts or, more cheaply, by arranging a fox-dig.[6] The course, usually of three to four miles, was a secret until start of the race, but it was not unknown for fences to have been holed to help a fancied horse through. Weights were supposedly 12 or 12.5 stone but, according to Robert Surtees the sporting writer, 'forget the scales, forget the weights' was more commonly the order of the day. He claimed that steeplechasing was so disreputably managed that few sportsmen would agree to act as stewards a second time.[7]

The date of the first Grand National is generally held to be 1839, although steeplechases were held at Aintree in 1836, 1837 and 1838. The event of 1839 was called the Grand Liverpool Steeplechase, changing to the Liverpool and National Steeplechase in 1843, and finally settling on its present-day name in 1847. In 1839 53 horses entered for a £20 stake, and there was £100 of added money. The horses carried their 12-stone riders over four miles. One horse was killed, Captain Becher fell into the brook that took his name and Jem Mason, one of steeplechasing's few professional jockeys, was the winner on *Lottery*. A horse later acquired by Lord Craven, *Charity*, also took part in this race, but refused a stone wall (inserted, supposedly, for the benefit of Irish entrants who were accustomed to them). Following her sale into Craven ownership *Charity* went on to win the 1841 Grand National at 14 to 1, beating *Lottery*,[8] although the triumph appears not to have been a matter of pride to Lord Craven, nor was it mentioned in

---

[6] MUNTING. *Hedges and hurdles.* p39
[7] SETH-SMITH. *History of steeplechasing.* p50
[8] SUFFOLK & BERKSHIRE. *Racing and steeplechasing.* p350

his obituary. Third place was taken by a horse belonging to his younger brother, the Hon. Frederick Craven.

Fig 14. William, second Earl of Craven (1809 - 1866), by Comte D'Orsay. Owner of Charity (Grand National winner 1841), co-owner of Wild Dayrell (Derby winner 1855), steward of the third Newbury steeplechase (1841) and a talented pioneer photographer.

Steeplechasing first reached west Berkshire also in 1839. The Newbury Maiden Steeplechase took place at noon on 26th March, and was open to horses from within a 20-mile radius. Four, five and six-year-olds would carry 10.5, 11.5 and 12 stone respectively. The prize was modest; £3 stakes with £25 of added money. Entries were to be made to Mr Elderfield at the White Hart in Newbury's Market Place. The following week the *Reading Mercury* carried a report by a writer who proudly claimed to know nothing of steeplechasing, but he counted 6,000 spectators, of whom 1,500 were mounted. Five runners set off from the gamekeeper's house at Sydmonton, a few miles south of Newbury, just across the border in Hampshire. They negotiated a three-and-a-half mile course over land belonging to Mr Paxton, finishing in the village then called Itchingswell (today it is called Ecchinswell) near Greenham Common. The winner was a horse called *Deception* which, according to the terms of the race, was then to be put up for auction, but the reporter omitted further details. He noted, however, that there was no loss of life or limb.[9]

Rather more space was allocated to reports of the second Newbury Steeplechase in March 1840, which the same newspaper introduced with the words 'this affair is creating a rich sensation in the sporting world'. This time the chase was to be open to all England, with all entrants carrying 12 stone, to be supplemented if the horse had won a steeplechase within the previous two years. Weighing-in would take place at the White Hart at 10 o'clock on the morning of the race. The winner would be put up for auction at £100. The prize money was raised to a £5 stake with £50 added, thanks to an anonymous donation supplemented by local 'gentlemen and inhabitants'. The stewards conformed to Flat custom by comprising a major and two esquires. The owners of the seven horses entered were plain misters. None was riding his own horse, and the seven jockeys, clearly a rung or two lower on the social ladder, were identified by their surnames only. [10]

Spectators were urged by handbill to stay off the course, and riders were exhorted to respect private land not included in the course, injunctions the *Reading Mercury* dubbed 'almost futile'. The three-and-three-quarter-mile route traversed farmland occupied by several named individuals, and included 40 banks, ditches, fences and waterways. In cold, dry weather the runners lined up in Mr Satchell's field by Enborne Gate Farm. Two failed even to start, whilst the other five took off over low-lying

---

[9] *RM* 16 and 30 March 1839
[10] *RM* 7 and 21 Mar 1840

meadows heading for Skinners Green. Here one refused a fence, and was not seen again. The others passed over fields of swede, where one horse was seen to clear a ditch in a 25-foot leap, and turned around Long Copse. Galloping eastwards towards Enborne Lodge (then the centre of a modest estate bordering Newbury's Wash Common) another horse bolted into oblivion. The three survivors careered down to Bunkers Hill, which was crowded with anxious spectators. Heading towards Wash Common, the field then turned south to cross the 20-foot wide River Enborne, finishing just over the Hampshire border. The winner (by a nose), jockey Vickers on Mr Price's *Old Billy*, had fallen and remounted three times. However there were no serious injuries, and the newspaper declared that 'a gayer scene we have not witnessed in the environs of Newbury for many a day'. Two hurdle races (one open, and one for locals) were scheduled to follow on Northcroft, the town commons, but the *Reading Mercury* reporter seems not to have bothered to attend these. The day's triumphs were celebrated over dinner afterwards at the White Hart.[11]

The event was clearly a success because it was repeated the following year on 26th March, this time with Lord Craven (the second earl) and George Willes (landowner and JP of Hungerford Park) joining the previous year's stewards. Lord Craven was officiating just three weeks after his horse *Charity* had won at Aintree, although the *Reading Mercury* makes no mention of this.

Spectators flooded in by cart and gig. In the absence of any grandstand they climbed trees in their Sunday best. This time the course ran broadly northwards through Enborne, finishing at Skinners Green. Those on horseback looked 'fully prepared to join the reckless train', suggesting that the Georgian tradition of a free-for-all in the final furlongs was far from dead. The runners included three owner-riders, one of whom was first past the post, but he was subsequently disqualified for not having kept the line. One horse had to be destroyed. A second, shorter, hunt steeplechase with three runners followed the main event, after which Northcroft was again the scene of some hurdle races. The proceedings closed once again with dinner at the White Hart.[12]

After these three apparently successful years no more is heard of the Newbury Steeplechase, for reasons which are unclear. Perhaps, in accordance with Robert Surtees' assertion, there were no more gentlemen prepared to act as stewards. Elsewhere however the sport was still growing

---

[11] *RM* 26 Mar 1840
[12] *RM* 20 Mar 1841

in popularity. Cheltenham had launched a steeplechase in 1841, and the Grand National (by now a handicap race) had secured a further £150 in prize money. In 1842 there were 66 such meetings in all England, as compared with just three in 1830.

Steeplechasing waned slightly in popularity during the Crimean War, when military energies were engaged elsewhere, but the sport was taken up in Reading by 1857 on a prepared course south of Whiteknights. These meetings were occasionally reported in *The Times*.[13] They ran over two days, each with three or four races. Added money ranged between £25 and £50 per race. The reports indicate no titled involvement, but the Duffields, a prominent hunting family descended from the Georgian landowner John Elwes, appear; Thomas Duffield rode his own horse to victory in a maiden of 1862.[14] Windsor too ran steeplechases intermittently from 1842. Here the race of 1861 was attended by Queen Victoria, who apparently left precipitately on overhearing some bad language from a jockey.[15]

By 1862 there was a rising clamour for regulation of steeplechasing, led by William George (W. G.) Craven, the racing writer and nephew of the second earl. As a long-serving member and steward of the Jockey Club, his commitment to Flat racing was unimpeachable, but he also campaigned strongly on behalf of steeplechasing. Like his uncle he had a Grand National runner. This was a horse called *Xanthus*, which came third in 1858 and 1860, and fifth in 1861. In 1866 W. G. Craven persuaded the Jockey Club to recognise the newly formed National Hunt Committee (NHC), on which he sat with, among others, Lord Poulett of Hackwood Park (Basingstoke's one-time racecourse) and Sir William Throckmorton of Buckland, near Faringdon. Through the NHC steeplechasing was finally regulated.

Hurdling too was brought under the NHC. Legend has it that a bored Prince of Wales once set his friends to jumping some sheep hurdles on the South Downs around 1810, thus giving rise to the sport. However, despite this supposedly royal origin, hurdling had long been derided by almost all the racing establishment as a test neither of pure speed, nor of serious jumping ability. The sport was considered to support bookies rather than bloodstock, and certainly it was always closely associated with gambling. However critics of hurdling perhaps underestimated its role in bridging the Flat and jump racing. Then as now, hurdling often served as a nursery of steeplechasing champions.

---

[13] *The Times* 30 Dec 1857
[14] *The Times* 28 Feb 1862
[15] BOYD. *Running horses*. p19

Fig 15. William George Craven (1835-1906). Eldest son of George Augustus Craven (who was 2nd son of the 1st earl) Jockey and owner of Flat horses and steeplechasers, Jockey Club member/steward and prominent writer on racing, active promoter of steeplechasing and co-founder of National Hunt Committee 1866.

Steeplechasing's heyday ran through the 1880s and 1890s, when Abingdon and Oxford joined Reading in the calendar. It continued to be a poor relation of the Flat in terms of fashion, wealth and aristocratic patronage, and was considered to be much less of a gambling focus. However a report in the *Newbury Weekly News* suggests that there was enough gambling to inflame local passions. Police had to rescue two defaulting bookies from a ducking in the river at a steeplechase meeting at Abingdon's Otney Meadows in 1884, and associated tensions erupted again later that night in town, leading to a four-hour street fight over which the police had little control. The rescued bookies, meanwhile, took a free train ride back to London by dint of conning passengers into giving up their tickets.[16]

Two more steeplechasing courses opened not far from Reading: Hawthorn Hill and Maiden Erleigh. Both had strong hunting and military associations. Hawthorn Hill, near Maidenhead, was established in 1887 chiefly for the purpose of recognising the co-operation of farmers in supporting the Royal Buckhounds. In 1888 a champagne luncheon was served to 500 farmers over whose land the Royal Buckhounds ran. A grandstand was borrowed from Egham racecourse for this event, but normally spectators took their chance in the open field. The same course hosted regimental steeplechases for the 12th Lancers, the Household Brigade and Royal Horse Guards in 1890. Maiden Erleigh was established as a joint hunt and military enterprise, and was said to attract 'a large concourse of Berkshire gentry'.[17]

Under NHC rules, published in 1874, steeplechasing become respectable and eventually professional. Meetings were now listed in the *Racing Calendar*. Courses were standardized on a minimum of three miles, with 12 fences in the first two miles (excluding hurdles) and at least six in each succeeding mile. There would be a water jump of 12-foot width and two-foot depth, guarded by a fence of not more than three-foot. In each mile there was to be a ditch six-foot wide and two-foot deep. Fences were not to exceed four-foot-six in height nor two-foot in width.[18] Some considered steeplechasing to have been thus tamed. One critic scorned the modern courses as 'attended to almost like tennis lawns or cricket pitches'.[19] However the newly respectable sport excluded the traditional hunting fraternity, who still wanted to race as amateurs, sometimes on the Flat but particularly across open country. Hunts increasingly organised their own race meetings of both kinds, but with scant reference to the now stringent conditions laid down by the Jockey Club, which had long since ceased to list hunt races. The Craven Hunt (which no longer involved the Craven family) held such a Flat meeting at Hungerford in 1870 for locals and members only, placing handicaps on thoroughbreds.

Lord Craven (George, the third earl, who succeeded to the title in 1866) was for many years joint master of the Old Berks Hunt with Tom

---

[16] *NWN* 24 Apr 1884
[17] *VCH Berks* vol ii p309
[18] BAYLES. *Racecourse atlas.* p113
[19] SETH-SMITH. *History of steeplechasing.* p70

Duffield (whose bad language in the field earned the hunt the nickname of the Old Blasphemers). An hospitable country squire of the old school, George Craven organised and hosted what seems to have been a one-off hunt race meeting entitled the Ashdown Diversions, held at his park near Lambourn in 1870. Nearly 3,000 spectators were estimated to be present, including a good turnout of local gentry: Cravens, Palks, Van der Weyers, Wroughtons and Duffields came in carriages, which were duly lined up alongside the track, and there was also a grandstand. (Lambourn still had no railway.) The Ashdown Diversions bore the hallmarks of a country race meeting of a century earlier, incorporating almost everything which was by then disapproved of by the Jockey Club. There was a give-and-take race for galloways, a pony match, a scurry, a hurdle race, prizes of saddles and bridles, and a plethora of owner-riders including Lord Craven, Tom Duffield and Philip Wroughton. Lord Craven promised that the event would be annual, but there was no repeat, possibly because the following year was overtaken by lavish civic celebrations of the wedding of Queen Victoria's daughter.[20]

Thereafter hunt race meetings in west Berkshire tended to be lower-profile steeplechases. The Old Berkshires met at Baulking on the downs in March 1872, where Lord Craven's horse broke its neck on a badly constructed water jump. It was the equine fatality which reached the pages of the *Newbury Weekly News* rather than the meeting itself, although the hunt's history claims 7,000 were present. Another Old Berks Hunt steeplechase took place at Coleshill, near Faringdon in 1881, under NHC rules. Lord Craven was both judge and steward, and his brother Osbert was clerk. Craven racing patronage seemed by now to have forsaken the Flat course for jumps.

By the 1890s point-to-point meetings, as they were now called, were being held by most of the local hunts. The season operated from January to June, with Easter weekend a favourite. Venues moved from year to year, with no permanently laid-out courses. These races were resolutely amateur, and entry was confined to active hunt members and participating farmers. Thoroughbred racehorses and professional jockeys were excluded. The Craven Hunt point-to-point of 1899 was probably typical. It was held south-west of Newbury, close to the ground that had been used for the Newbury Steeplechases of half a century earlier. Both the start and finish were conveniently sited together, by Gore End Bridge, and a contemporaneous account describes carts, carriages and horsemen lined up over 100 yards at

---

[20] *NWN* 10 Mar 1870

this point, as well as spectators along the route, which stretched back into Hamstead Marshall. The first race, over three-and-a-half miles of mostly meadow, was for *bona fide* hunt members, and a second was for farmers. No horse which had won under NHC (professional steeplechasing) rules was eligible. Two bookies put in an appearance, but the reporter doubted that there had been enough business to warrant their rail tickets from London.[21]

---

[21] *NWN* 6 Apr 1899

7

The new professions
Trainers, touts and jockeys

Very early one morning in April 1852 a colt foal was born at Littlecote, seat of the Popham family, many generations of whom had supported racing at Marlborough and Newbury. It was the first foaling at Francis Popham's stud, and it was duly celebrated with a bottle of wine. A decision was then taken to move the foal to a warmer box, a task which the butler performed with a wheelbarrow, declaring that he would like the unique opportunity of transporting a future Derby winner.

His prophecy proved correct. *Wild Dayrell,* as the foal was named (after a notorious member of the family which had formerly owned Littlecote) won the 1855 Derby for his joint owners, Francis Popham and Lord Craven (the second earl, who had also owned the 1841 Grand National winner *Charity*). The story of *Wild Dayrell's* birth, training and eventual Derby triumph may have acquired some extra polish over the years, but it undoubtedly encapsulates a turning point in English horse-racing history, when the leisurely interest of genial country squires ran up against hard-nosed professionals and keen commercialism.

Popham's bloodstock enterprise was a dilettante pastime rather than a serious, market-oriented operation. Notwithstanding the butler's confidence in *Wild Dayrell*, the horse was sold, and moved to Goodwood, where he failed to show promise. When the two-year-old fetched up at Tattersalls with nothing to his credit, Popham bought him back, sharing ownership with his friend and neighbour Lord Craven. *Wild Dayrell* trained first on the Littlecote estate about 10 miles west of Newbury, and later on the downland turf of the Craven estate at Ashdown, under Popham's groom, Rickaby. He raced once that season, winning at Newmarket. Subsequent trials revealed his potential, and he was entered for the 1855 Derby.

So far so amateur, but racing's shadier element became involved. As a heavily fancied Derby runner *Wild Dayrell* continued to be offered at curiously generous odds. The word amongst bookies was that the horse would be 'settled' before the race. His innocently unsuspecting owners were alerted when covertly offered £5,000 to withdraw the horse. Further shenanigans at the Ashdown yard led to dismissal of a stable boy, and the implementation of unprecedented security. A horse-drawn van intended to transport the contender to Epsom collapsed violently when subjected to trial with a bullock inside. Eventually the race went ahead as planned, with (by now) even money on *Wild Dayrell*, which won by two comfortable lengths.[1]

Fig 16. Wild Dayrell, 1855 Derby winner co-owned by Francis Popham and Lord Craven. Photographed by Lord Craven, with Ashdown House in the background. The man in the top hat is probably Lord Craven's groom/trainer Rickaby.

Francis Popham was deeply disillusioned, and declared his withdrawal from Derby racing. Nonetheless, he had made local history by providing Berkshire with its first Derby winner. Lord Craven, whose involvement was rather less documented, was responsible for another first; as a keen early photographer he turned his lens onto *Wild Dayrell* at Ashdown, thus creating the first photograph of a Derby winner. The racing establishment

---

[1] MORTIMER. *History of Derby Stakes.* passim

however was scandalised that such a victory could have been gained by an amateur. They regarded the 1855 Derby as something of a throwback. Professional trainers were by now considered to have replaced the trusted grooms of private stables, such as Rickaby.

The rise of the public trainer had been no overnight sensation. The profession evolved gradually alongside the professional jockey and, later, professional racecourse officials. Early private trainers evolved from stud grooms and, as servants, they were not always credited for their successes; Rickaby's Christian name is not on record, and throughout the first half of the nineteenth century there are gaps in the records for the St Leger and the 2,000 Guineas, in which it was not thought important or appropriate to note the trainer's name.

Independent trainers appeared in the 1820s. Some were private insofar as they worked exclusively for one or perhaps two owners; later the public trainer emerged from their ranks, taking horses from all-comers. Their status in relation to their clients was at first ambiguous. The old association with stable grooms lingered, holding trainers in the servant class. Racehorse training was not at first considered to be a gentleman's occupation, although the trainer was socially superior to the jockey. Over the middle years of the nineteenth century trainers took on a more managerial role, and the shift to professional status occurred. By the end of the century they were a solidly middle-class profession, including both gentlemen and ex-jockeys in their ranks. Robert Peck, the prominent trainer resident at Russley Park in the 1870s and 1880s, even had his own coachman.[2]

Trainers were sometimes not trusted, because their interests might not always coincide with those of their clients. They were not supposed to bet, although some did, pleading necessity on the grounds that racehorse owners tended to be slow payers. However the general opinion of the time was that, by and large, trainers were more dependably honest than most other interest groups in racing.[3] The Jockey Club made no move to regulate them until late in the century.

The racehorse training benefits of East Ilsley's downland had of course been recognised by the Duke of Cumberland a century earlier, and the activity had continued in the area after he left.[4] However the full potential of the downland to the north and south of Newbury (the Berkshire and Hampshire downs) came to more prominent notice in the mid-

---

[2] 1881 census
[3] VAMPLEW. *Turf.* p175
[4] HEWETT. *History and antiquities of the hundred of Compton in Berks.* p59-60

nineteenth century, when Newmarket underwent a series of dry summers, and trainers urgently sought more forgiving ground. The springy turf of the chalk downs defied all extremes of weather, and the gently rolling hills proved excellent for the development of good muscle. The 1851 census for Berkshire enumerated eight training establishments dotted along the line of the Ridgeway from East Ilsley to Letcombe Regis, and another four in the east of Berkshire.

In 1851 Ilsley's largest establishment was based upon the Swan Inn, where Newbury-born George Drewe operated as victualler and trainer. (The combination of victualling with an unrelated trade was quite common.) The census recorded no fewer than 20 'trainer's servants' at this address, and in his employ. Fourteen of them were 18 years old or under, with the three youngest being 12. Only three were local, the remainder having come from all over the country. Thomas Stevens had a smaller establishment in Broad Street. The son of a Gloucestershire trainer who had set up a yard in Ilsley in the 1830s, Stevens had 11 'trainer's servants'.

Third in size was the Abingdon Road yard of Mathew Dawson, one of four brothers who were all to become successful trainers. Here the census recorded five stable lads (two from near Newmarket, and three from Yorkshire) and a visiting jockey from Manchester.

Lambourn first attracted trainers in the late 1840s. In the 1851 census three yards were enumerated, the largest being that of Edwin Parr, by then in his late 50s. Parr employed eight lads, of which two were jockeys and the remainder grooms. Next in size was trainer John King with three jockey lads. Another trainer, William Ford, appears to have been a solo operator.[5]

The 1881 census shows a significant increase in the number of training stables and an increase in average establishment size over 30 years. Four yards within a 20-mile radius of Newbury now employed 20 or more, and four more employed between 10 and 20. East Ilsley's biggest yard was now that of James Dover, who had arrived in 1862. His yard at Churchill Cottage produced several classic winners, including *Lord Lyon*, which in 1866 won the Triple Crown of the 2,000 Guineas, the Derby and the St Leger. (*Lord Lyon* belonged to Richard Sutton, son of the owner of Benham Park, and it was into this lush landscape that the horse was turned loose to enjoy his well-earned retirement.) The following year *Achievement*, from the same yard, won the 1,000 Guineas and the St Leger. By 1881 Dover was employing 20 stablemen, but the establishment later foundered when taken over by his son.

---

[5] 1851 census

Thomas Stevens, whom the 1851 census had found in East Ilsley with 11 employees, was by 1881 at Lime Tree Cottage in Chilton, presiding over a dynasty of four sons who were training locally, 17 stablemen and jockeys.

Lambourn's largest stableyard was Seven Barrows, to which Charles Jousiffe came in 1877, leasing 532 acres from the Craven estate. Jousiffe's racing career began with a jockey apprenticeship in England, followed by 11 years riding and training in India. By 1881 he was employing 12 lads and five men at Seven Barrows.[6] As the private trainer for three owners, Jousiffe sent out many winners, the most famous of which was *Bendigo*, whose winnings of more than £30,000 were popularly claimed to have paid for a new lychgate for Lambourn churchyard, where Jousiffe was buried in 1891.[7]

In eastern Wiltshire Russley Park stables, near Bishopstone, were pre-eminent. Horses from this yard used the nearby Lambourn downs for training. In the 1860s the premises were rented from the Craven estate by James Merry, a dour Scottish ironmaster whose plebeian origins earned him a degree of condescension from the racing aristocracy. He was, however, a successful owner and heavy better. At Russley Park he installed as trainer Mathew Dawson, who sent out Merry's 1860 Derby winner, *Thormanby*. Robert Peck took over the yard in 1872, when Dawson moved on to Newmarket. Merry's horses remained there until his retirement from the Turf in 1875. Here in 1881, the census found 17 stablemen, jockeys and apprentices working under Robert Peck.

Another training establishment recorded in the 1881 census was Manton House, built on the edge of Marlborough Downs in 1870. Here Alexander Taylor presided over a massive complement of 42 stable lads. Ten Classic winners were sent out from here in 24 years.[8] The village of Wroughton, near Swindon, was home to three much smaller establishments.

Two major training establishments lay to the south of Newbury in the Hampshire downs. Kingsclere had been the training choice of the infamous Counsellor Lade and his namesake Sir John Lade in the late eighteenth century. In the mid-nineteenth century their former base of Cannon Park operated as the yard of Sir Joseph Hawley, a dictatorial owner, who installed John Porter as his private trainer in 1860. Cannon Park was replaced by Park House yard in 1867, newly built at Hawley's expense and to Porter's detailed specification. It was a model yard in every sense, including positively

[6] 1881 census
[7] *Sporting Life* 27 Feb 1891
[8] *VCH Wilts* vol iv p382

sumptuous accommodation for stable lads.[9] Superb gallops were laid out on Watership Down, including a stretch known as the Derby gallop, sited well out of the view of touts. Thanks to a generous clause in Hawley's will, Porter was able to buy the yard on his master's death in 1875. From here he sent out a nearly 1,000 winners for the Prince of Wales, the dukes of Portland and Westminster and other luminaries of late nineteenth-century racing. Nonetheless, Porter claimed that training fees had not enriched him, but merely ensured his subsistence, whilst his savings had been modestly amassed from gifts from grateful patrons, and some successful speculations in bloodstock.[10]

Fig 17. Park House yard, Kingsclere, in 1895.

Stockbridge, a sleepy village on the river Test in north-western Hampshire, had both a racecourse and a strong training tradition. Three generations of the Day family ran the yard here, first at Houghton House and then at Danebury, an establishment of stables and gallops over 2,340 acres, much of it subsidised by Lord George Bentinck. The Danebury yard trained Bentinck's filly *Crucifix*, which won both the 1,000 Guineas and the

[9] VAMPLEW. *Turf.* p154
[10] PORTER. *Kingsclere.* p18-19

2,000 Guineas of 1840. Shortly after this Bentinck fell out with John Day, and removed his horses to Goodwood. The future prime minister Lord Palmerston also kept his horses at Danebury which, at its peak, housed 70 horses. In the 1881 census the yard listed five stablemen, 13 apprentice trainers and two stableman trainers under John Day and his son Leonard. The former jockey Tom Cannon later married John Day's daughter, and in 1893 took over Danebury. It is from this dynasty that Lester Piggott is descended.

Notwithstanding the spread of railways from 1840, the best training locations tended to be the most remote. 'Five miles from anywhere' was John Porter's ideal. Such isolation had its downside; until the arrival of the railway branch line in 1898, Lambourn-trained horses had to be walked 10 miles to the nearest GWR station at Uffington, East Ilsley's a similar distance to Steventon.[11] A slightly shorter trudge took Kingsclere horses to the station at Overton.

However such remote locations had the attraction (to trainers) of keeping impressionable young stable lads beyond the reach of pubs and touts, who were renowned for suborning gullible apprentices with beer, bribes and bullying.

A tout might work for a tipster paper or for a rival owner, obtaining confidential information about the performance and condition of horses. They were the bane of trainers' lives regarded, according to John Porter, much as the gamekeeper regards the poacher. He boasted of horsewhipping one for making approaches to one of his stable staff, and the incident was by no means untypical. Derby hopefuls had to be kept under sleepless surveillance. Despite his 'invisible' Derby gallop, Porter claimed that news of his training progress was consistently and accurately reported in the racing press, implying that it was impossible to plug information leaks even from his own employees.[12]

'The Lambourn Lynx, never seen but always seeing', was one who wrote for the tipster press in the 1860s. The 1881 census confirms this new racing occupation; two residents of Upper Lambourn (a tiny hamlet) described themselves as sports reporters, but their presence in Upper Lambourn speaks more of spying on the nearby gallops than reporting from distant racecourses.

During the second quarter of the nineteenth century off-course betting was becoming endemic amongst ordinary working men. Incomes

---

[11] BOYD. 'Sport of kings and queens.' *Berkshire Family Historian* (June 2002) p220-24
[12] PORTER. *Kingsclere.*

and leisure were increasing. Cash bets of sixpence or a shilling were the norm, placed with 'list men', who worked through pubs, those same establishments which also promoted sweepstakes. The later nineteenth century witnessed an explosion in racing newspapers, such as the *Racing Times* and *Racing Telegraph.* These publications were betting-oriented, and aimed at ordinary punters – a new readership which never attended the racecourse, and could not afford the ten shillings which tipsters charged for more 'exclusive' information.

The Betting House Act of 1853 outlawed all off-course cash betting premises, targeting this pub trade. Upper-class punters could continue to bet legally on credit at Tattersalls, and a further substantial volume of upmarket gambling business was taken overseas to avoid prosecution. But such remedies were not for the ordinary punter. Although ignored with some degree of impunity for a while, the new law gradually extinguished pub-based betting, giving rise to the street-corner bookie, always on the lookout for the approaching constable. The application of the Act to racecourses was more ambiguous, and betting survived here, albeit under frequent challenge.[13]

The honesty of street bookies is a matter for speculation. Certainly before the advent of the electric telegraph it would have been relatively easy to swindle gamblers who had no way of checking results or odds. Both the government and the Jockey Club had abdicated from betting in the 1840s (when gaming debts were made non-recoverable at law), so there were profits to be made from ignorant punters, and one notable scam was based in Kingsclere. William Walter, son of the landlady of the Swan, published the *Kingsclere Racing Circular,* a tipster publication. Walter, who used several aliases and alternative addresses, promoted a scheme for 'investment' to 'insure' against turf losses. The fraud was roundly denounced in the *Sporting Times* in 1870, and the following year Walter was fined for keeping a betting house. He was hauled into court again in 1875, and finally sentenced to 20 years for fraud.[14]

From 1871 the *Sporting Chronicle* began to publish starting prices, and the old practice of 'play-or-pay', whereby bets on non-runners were lost, was abandoned. Such cleaning up of potential abuse was welcome, but it also served to encourage more gambling, or so was claimed by John Porter specifically for his home village of Kingsclere.[15]

---

[13] ITZKOWITZ . p7-30
[14] PORTER. *Kingsclere.* p 66, 317, 321-23
[15] HUGGINS, *Flat racing.* p103

Professional jockeys had been around since the 1790s, and from 1810 were gradually replacing amateurs in the saddle. For big races the advantage of lightweight professionals was clear, and none of the five Classic races was ever won by an amateur. Owner-riders, amateurs and gentleman jockeys (most of whom were unable and/or unwilling to reduce to seven stone) persisted only in racing backwaters, of which there were still several in west Berkshire. Abingdon had several races for gentleman riders in 1855 and 1857 (professional jockeys being allotted extra weight), as did Hungerford in 1860, and Lambourn's meeting in 1865 must surely have been one of the last sightings of the species. In 1879 the Jockey Club introduced a licensing system for jockeys, which sealed the exclusion of amateurs from mainstream Flat racing. Gentleman riders took refuge first in steeplechasing, and when that too professionalised, eventually in point-to-point races.

Jockeys were at first regarded as socially lowly by the racing élite, and it was customary not to bother with their Christian names or initials in race reports. Their earnings reflected their social status; three guineas for a race, or five if they won. However it was generally expected that wins would be supplemented with a gift, which could be substantial if the owner was generous. Sir Joseph Hawley delighted in thumbing his nose at the disapproving Jockey Club (with whom he was often in dispute) by giving prize money to jockeys – in the case of the 1868 Derby, the entire prize of about £6,000.[16] James Merry, by way of contrast, gave jockey Henry Custance just £100 from his £6,350 winnings on the Lambourn-trained *Thormanby* in the 1860 Derby.[17] In later years, a select few jockeys became celebrities, fêted in high society, and commanding stupendous earnings. Contempt for 'skinny dwarfs whose leaders are paid better than the greatest statesmen'[18] was the choleric reaction of the die-hard aristocrats, who saw the potential inversion of society as celebrity jockeys were welcomed into upper-class salons.

Even as late as the 1870s some of these famous jockeys made regular appearances on west Berkshire's few remaining meetings. Most celebrated of all was Fred Archer (1857 - 1886), who came from Cheltenham, and was apprenticed aged 11 to Mathew Dawson. He is still acknowledged by many

---

[16] VAMPLEW. *Turf.* p145-6
[17] HUGGINS, *Flat racing.* p162
[18] RUNCIMAN. 'Ethics of the turf.' *Contemporary Review* (1889) p607-8

to be the best all-round jockey the Turf has ever seen. John Porter frequently employed him. In his earlier career, before he became an adulated star of the premier league, Archer also rode at relatively humble meetings, such as Odiham (where, late into the nineteenth century, some prizes were still in kind rather than cash) and at Lambourn in 1877, by which time he already had over 200 wins to his credit. The Lambourn appearance was probably connected with his fondness for hunting with the Old Berkshires. George Fordham was another nationally famous jockey who sometimes appeared at local country courses. At Abingdon in 1855 and East Ilsley in 1857 he rode at meetings which included owner-riders. He also rode at Stockbridge for John Day.

The desire for light weight, combined with the lack of regulation, frequently led to children being placed in the saddle. Before the 1870 Education Act apprenticeships could begin at 11 years old, the age at which Fred Archer won his first race. The early professional jockeys tended to be urban and working-class, often underweight from malnutrition rather than being of genuinely small build. Once ensconced in a prosperous training stable, many fattened out on good country food. There was thus a high attrition rate in their numbers. Charles Jousiffe weighed five stone when first indentured as an apprentice jockey. Thereafter he struggled to remain under seven stone, when his natural weight would probably have been nearer eleven. In later life, as a prosperous Lambourn trainer, he weighed over sixteen stone. Fred Archer submitted to a gruelling regimen of Turkish baths and purgatives, the destabilizing effects of which were considered to have been contributory to his tragic suicide at the height of his success in 1886.

The Jockey Club's rise to national power was slow as to be almost imperceptible. Indeed, the point by which the club might reasonably be described as the governing body of racing is disputed by historians. Clearly it was an evolutionary process, which by 1850 had gained impetus from increasing concern for racing's dubious reputation. The club's response was a series of edicts restricting some of the more questionable activities of racecourse officials and jockeys. Lord George Bentinck's dual flag starts introduced in 1844 ended the chaos and abuse of more primitive methods. In 1848 presents to judges were banned, and in 1855 Admiral Rous was appointed public handicapper, ending some widespread anomalies. In 1866 the club decreed that fees should not be levied against winners (an unpopular means of fund-raising practised by many racecourses, including all of those in west Berkshire, but not Ascot). Following the licensing of jockeys in 1879 (largely on the initiative of W. G. Craven), in 1882 both jockeys and judges were banned from covert ownership of racehorses.[19]

The club had no means of enforcing these professional standards beyond its own remit of Newmarket, but the more forward-looking and successful racecourses were already adopting the new regulations. Ascot and Epsom had employed Jockey Club stewards and operated under Rules since the 1830s. In 1832 the club announced that it would no longer adjudicate disputes at courses which did not follow its rules,[20] but this seems to have been only partially implemented; such interventions were obtained at Ilsley, Hungerford and Abingdon after 1850, at meetings which were most decidedly non-JC. However, in general those courses that persisted with local rules and idiosyncratic practices stood out in sharp relief.

[19] SUFFOLK & BERKSHIRE. *Racing and steeplechasing.* p105-6
[20] HUGGINS. *Flat racing.* p178

8

The slow death of country racing
Social upheaval, mass transport and hard economics of 1830-1870

The post-Napoleonic War years proved harder for country racing. Newbury Races folded in 1815, whilst in 1813 Reading Races lapsed for 30 years. Abingdon and Ascot were the only consistent performers in Berkshire during the first half of the nineteenth century. In Oxfordshire only Port Meadow continued running after the war years, and this became fitful after 1842. In Wiltshire several minor courses failed as did Marlborough after 1811. In this year the Marlborough meeting transferred to Burderop for 20 years, folded for another decade, and then came back to Marlborough. Salisbury was the sole consistent performer in this county. The Hampshire courses of Basingstoke, Odiham, Southampton and Winchester were intermittent; Stockbridge was perhaps the strongest here.

However the decline was not universal. Some apparently defunct courses revived briefly. East Ilsley reopened for another two decades of racing in 1849. Banbury, Bicester and Burford had sporadic meetings, and a few minor Hampshire racecourses made fleeting appearances in the *Racing Calendar*. Hungerford, an entirely new name, flourished for two separate decades in mid-century. [1]

But in the longer term nearly all the country courses foundered. This process was influenced by a complex web of economic and social influences, some broad and others highly specific. The rise of professionalism, described in the last chapter, was already eroding the essentially amateur and local character of country race meetings. Furthermore, English society as a whole was undergoing a significant upheaval, in which traditional relationships and attitudes were being remoulded by Victorian middle-class mores. Both incomes and leisure time were on the increase amongst ordinary people. The railways opened up the possibility (for spectators and horses) of racing far from home. The Jockey Club finally found its place as an effective regulator. Although many local racecourses closed down for apparently specific local reasons, such as the death of a pivotal organiser, or

---

[1] A chart detailing the operational years of each course can be found in Appendix 2.

the withdrawal of facilities by a new landowner, there was eventually no place for old-style country racing in the new climate of a professional, commercial and national sport.

The catalyst in speeding the transformation of racing from local to a national sport was the railway. In west Berkshire these connections were relatively slow to establish. The Great Western Railway arrived in Reading in 1840, but it was to be another seven years before Newbury and Hungerford were linked by branch line, and Marlborough took a decade longer. Brunel's decision to take his main line to the north of the downs, through Didcot and Swindon, rather than through the Kennet valley, was partly due to the opposition from local landowners, who viewed the railway as a threat to their canal interests.[2] The Craven and Dundas estates refused to sell land to the GWR, hoping thus to escape its competition, but their protest was self-defeating. The main line simply bypassed the Kennet valley, and within a few years it still destroyed the canal trade, as it also wiped out the London to Bath coach trade. As road transport declined, so did the turnpikes. The formerly well-maintained roads fell into disrepair, which in turn drove traffic onto the railway. Newbury, Hungerford and Marlborough, whose economies were closely woven into road traffic, suffered badly.

Abingdon Races struggled on through mid-century without the benefit of a railway connection. Thomas Duffield of Marcham Park successfully obstructed a plan to link Steventon and Oxford via Abingdon, as a result of which the town did not gain a spur line until 1873.[3] However, this long-awaited benefit did not prevent the closure of Abingdon's long series two years later. The *Victoria County History* attributed the demise of Abingdon Races in 1875 to the death of the clerk Charles Cox,[4] but it is difficult to believe that more than a century of successful racing might have ended for this reason alone. Steeplechasing continued on Otney Meadows, but the racecourse on Abingdon Common was no longer the pride of the county.

---

[2] MONEY. *Popular history of Newbury.* p108
[3] McGOWAN. *Abingdon-Radley branch railway line.*
[4] *VCH Berks* vol ii p307

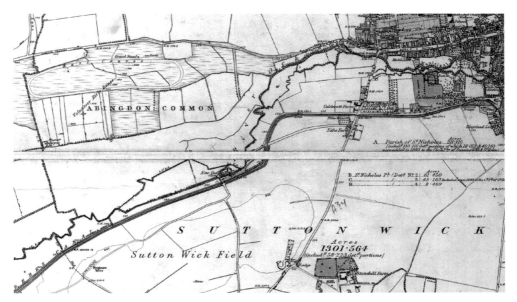

Fig 18. Abingdon Racecourse (top left) mapped in the 1880s, a decade after racing had officially ceased.

Reading Races were in abeyance when the GWR first linked the town with London. Within three years of the line opening the races revived at a new location in Kings Meadow, and an account of the 1844 meeting in the *Illustrated London News* extolled the renewed gaiety of festivities consisting of one day's regatta and two days' racing. The impression given was of a town rescued from the social doldrums, enjoying a fresh and sophisticated rebirth. There was, however, no mention of aristocratic patronage; the meeting seems to have originated in the town's trading interests. The article was accompanied by picture of the 1844 races at Reading, depicting a fashionable crowd, whose attention is wholly captured by events on the track. In the foreground of the picture, unnoticed by the cheering racegoers, a dubious-looking trio lugs away a striped booth as though intent upon a hasty and unobserved exit. Their business is unclear, but their determination to escape under cover of a rowdy race finish is unmistakeable. Perhaps Reading's new series still hosted some of the shadier, old-style, racecourse enterprise.

---

[5] *Illustrated London News* 31 Aug 1844

Fig. 19 Reading Races in 1844.

East Ilsley's brief racing resurgence of 1849 - 1858 also lacked railway support. The Didcot, Newbury and Southampton railway, taking in the village, did not open until 1882. Nonetheless the opening race meeting of 1849 featured a 'Railway Stakes' with £15 of added money, presumably from the GWR. This series, which ran until 1858, lacked noble patronage. Most of the added money seems to have come from the Old Berks Hunt, local trainers (a growing body) and gentlemen of the town.

Lambourn's spasmodic revival of racing in 1865 and the late 1870s was another which took place independently of rail communications, because the Lambourn Valley branch line from Newbury, first mooted in 1873, was not completed until 1898. (Hence the need for a horse-drawn van to transport *Wild Dayrell* to Epsom for the Derby in 1855.)

Hungerford first entered the *Racing Calendar* in 1840, seven years before the railway arrived. A racecourse was laid out on the Port Down common to the east of the town. There was a temporary grandstand, and the course, marked out each year, measured more than a mile around, although it was noted that the irregularity of the ground made results difficult to forecast. At this time it was considered that Hungerford Races would attract much bigger crowds once the town was connected by rail, but in 1849, two years after the GWR arrived, the meeting failed. A second series began in 1859 with, as Hazlitt might have observed, the Cockneys no longer distanced, but the resulting influx appears to have been mixed. Along with *bona fide* racegoers the railways transported travelling gangs of criminals who worked the racecourse crowds. There was trouble at Hungerford Races in 1868, and in 1869 there was a series of thefts, including that of the race promoter's dog-cart, followed by its brazen re-sale in Hungerford's High Street.[6] London was popularly supposed to be the source of racecourse gangs, but two pickpockets caught at the 1869 meeting turned out to be from Birmingham and Sheffield.[7] Beset by crime, scheduling problems and a course which could neither be improved nor made permanent because of common rights, Hungerford Races ceased to be listed after 1869. More informal and irregular meetings of plebeian racing continued, but these were beneath the attention of the *Racing Calendar*.

---

[6] BOYD. *Running horses.* p17
[7] *NWN* 2 Sep 1869

In the east of the county Ascot, never a typically country racecourse because of its overwhelmingly upper-class patronage, was nonetheless the type of racecourse which could and did benefit commercially from the railway's arrival. In 1856 the Staines-to-Wokingham line brought the racecourse within comfortable day-tripping distance from London, previously Epsom's monopoly. The increased attendance was unwelcome to the old guard. The influx of Cockneys was deplored, and there was much snobbish tittering in the press about the social shortcomings of the new clientèle.[8]

Fig 20. Ascot Racecourse mapped in 1880s. Unlike most Berkshire racecourses it has occupied the same site throughout its existence over the centuries.

It might almost be said that such prosperity as was enjoyed by west Berkshire's racecourses at this time was despite, rather than because of the railways. Rail travel released racegoers from the tie to locality, and the choice which they could exercise would only benefit the more forward-looking, entrepreneurial racecourses which wooed them. The 1869 meeting at Hungerford clashed with York Races, which would scarcely have been a problem in the pre-railway era, but it was noted by the *Newbury Weekly News* as having reduced attendance, indicating the distance that racegoers

---

[8] MAGEE. *Ascot*. p92-3

would now travel in search of a good day's sport. Their apparent willingness to shun west Berkshire's courses testifies to the area's backwardness in developing the sport.

It should be remembered that at this point there were still no turnstiles, and gate-money had yet to be a source of racecourse revenue. Many courses were on common land with full public right of access: Abingdon, Hungerford, Marlborough, Oxford and Southampton for example. No enclosure or even investment would come to such locations, and on such courses race meetings were doomed to remain free local festivals, dependent upon a traditional local assembly of mixed sexes, ages and classes. The post-1850 racegoer however was more likely to be a newly mobile, working-class male, a more knowledgeable and dedicated follower of a national sport, and the courses which ultimately prospered were those which upgraded to meet his enhanced expectations. The railway companies were quick to identify this market, and offered excursion packages to the more prestigious meetings. Such courses were flourishing fixtures when gate-money was introduced in the last quarter of the century.

Other factors conspired to undermine the viability of local racing. Easier transport lessened the need for racegoers to stay locally overnight, and thus the balls, concerts and theatricals which had been an integral part of race-week festivities lost support. In any case the new breed of racegoer was less interested in such diversions. Publicans had less to gain from subscription to race prize funds. Civic and social life associated with the old-style, country town race week suffered.

Country gentry ceased to take a kindly interest in their local courses. Those who had done so formerly out of *noblesse oblige* and a sense of commitment to community had no rapport with racegoers arriving by railway from a distant town. Even those of the upper classes who remained committed to racing disliked railways because they provided insufficient class segregation. They shunned them for as long as they could, and their horse-drawn carriages continued to line the racetrack for a while. One scarcely believable account alleges that in the early days of the railway, rather than occupy a public compartment, a gentleman would have his carriage hoisted up on to a railway truck, therein to wobble precariously in transit, 'till the manifest dangers of the system became patent'.[9] Such heroic obscurantism may make for hilarious history, but it also illustrates the reactionary attitudes that permeated the backwaters of the sport, and which contributed to country racing's demise.

---

[9] FOWLER. *Echoes of old country life.* p218

In these central southern counties the country landowners seem to have retained some hold on their social status despite their declining fortunes, at least until mid-century. At Abingdon's two-day meeting of 1839 most of the races were still named after local grand houses – Marcham Park, Woolley Park, Pusey, Holme Park, Buckland – implying current gentry sponsorship. This nomenclature was unusual even then. Not many race cards were still making such overt acknowledgment of personal patronage. As late as the 1840s the departure of the Marchioness of Ailesbury from Marlborough Races would be marked by her stately progress down the track, attended by outriders.[10] Such deferential ceremony was increasingly a rarity at racecourses. Apart from Ascot, where the royal parade instituted by George IV had become a popular tradition under Queen Victoria, the old-style parades of gentry had been replaced by parades of horses and jockeys, indicating a more professional focus to the proceedings.

Berkshire landowning families felt the pinch in the second half of the nineteenth century. Their agricultural interests were threatened by imported grain, and successful farming now called for heavy investment in new technology. There was little to spare for racehorse-owning, the costs of which had in any case spiralled. It has been estimated that the overall proportion of titled owners reduced from one-third in 1830 to one-eighth in 1890.[11] Only the super-rich nobility remained in racing. Their one-time dominance of racehorse ownership was now shared with syndicates and a new plutocracy (typified by James Merry) with no specifically local roots.

Even the once-mighty Craven family fortune was under pressure. The second earl inherited around 57,000 acres in 1825, but with fearsome encumbrances. Whilst he dabbled in racing (*Charity* and *Wild Dayrell*, and a one-off meeting at Ashdown in 1865), the requirement for careful estate management precluded any Turf extravagance on the scale of his forebears. For the first time since its foundation, Jockey Club membership did not include the Craven title-holder. This second earl's interests were the more modern pursuits of yachting and photography.[12] His son, who became the third earl in 1866, was more of a traditional field sportsman, and relished the simple pleasures of country squiredom. In this role he presided over Lambourn's brief racing revival in the 1870s, but his son and successor in

---

[10] *VCH Wilts* vol iv p381
[11] VAMPLEW. *Turf* p178
[12] CRAVEN. unpublished family memoir.

1883, the fourth earl, did not even live in west Berkshire, and took no interest in racing.[13]

As the upper classes retired from influencing rural society, the vacuum was filled by a militant middle class intent upon improving their social inferiors. Cockfighting and prizefighting were now illegal, and race meetings were already shedding other dubious activities. Oxford forbade gambling tables and all sideshows at Port Meadow except Punch and Judy,[14] and a *Berkshire Chronicle* advertisement of 1843 made clear that Abingdon races would be free of gambling booths. However, though cleansed of bloodsports and the more blatant frauds, racing still failed to dislodge its association with crime, sexual licence, drunkenness, brawling and, of course, the moral evil of gambling. Betting, which spread rapidly among the working class from 1840, was widely blamed for absenteeism, theft, damage to family life and immiseration.

However the extent to which racegoing was shunned in practice by the Victorian moralisers is disputed, one hypothesis being that at least some of the middle classes were obsessed with a sport that exemplified their social aspirations, but was beyond their reach.[15] 'I can't afford a thoroughbred and can't abide a cocktail,'[16] wailed Thackeray's status-conscious creation, George, in the *Fitz-Boodle Papers* of 1842. However if respectable men did go to the races more than they cared to admit, it also seems that respectable Victorian women could not enjoy racegoing as freely as did their Georgian predecessors. A social lead may have been taken from Queen Victoria, who attended Ascot as a matter of duty, but was known to be indifferent to and ignorant about the sport. A study of Victorian racing art has estimated women spectators to be depicted in no more than 10 per cent of the crowd.[17] Women as racehorse-owners are a rarity by the mid-nineteenth century, although one notable exception who raced at Reading was Mrs. Osbaldeston, wife of the eccentric sportsman squire.

The reformist tendency found expression in moral broadsides against racing from the evangelical clergy. At first high-church Anglicans were less ready to condemn; many parsons were still riding to hounds and racegoing. Walter Money vividly described an 1820s painting of the Craven Hunt, in which four local clergymen were prominent among the gentry in

---

[13] Craven family racing interests 1750-1900 are tabulated in Appendix 1.
[14] CORDEAUX & MERRY. p63
[15] FILBY. *Sociology of horse racing in Britain.* p67
[16] A cocktail was a horse of mixed breeding.
[17] HUGGINS. *Flat racing.* p120

the saddle.[18] Later in the century (by which time Berkshire was in the Oxford diocese) the Bishop of Oxford, Samuel Wilberforce, stoutly declared a sporting clergyman to be 'a great evil in a parish'.[19]

He no doubt approved of the Rev. Robert Milman, incumbent of Lambourn in the 1850s. Milman was an admirer of manly sports, but he did not count racing among them, and he forbade the popular village custom of ringing the church bells to celebrate a local win. This culminated in the truculent bellringers locking themselves in the tower to ensure a peal in honour of *Wild Dayrell* in 1855. Milman's biographer claimed that he was however the ultimate victor in the stand-off, by virtue of a vehement sermon which was said to have cowed the miscreants.[20]

At Burford racing had been traditional in the village since the days of Charles II, although since the departure of the Bibury Club in 1802 meetings had been intermittent and uncalendared. However in 1859 the vicar of Aldsworth (the parish of Burford's racecourse) exterminated this, along with a whole gamut of sinful village pleasures. He was credited with 'abolishing the races, banning the stables, suppressing public houses, closing shops on Sundays and putting an end to Sunday games, sports, wrestling, boxing, cockfighting and cricket which had been usual on the village green'.[21] The power of Victorian clergy to direct social life seems scarcely credible today.

Whilst parsons thundered from the pulpit, some evangelicals actually ventured onto the Turf to turn racegoers away from sin. An organization called the Open Air Mission (still in existence today) was renowned for taking the gospel to race meetings, and 12 such missionaries attended Reading Races in 1856. Their report was dubiously upbeat, claiming a favourable reception from the public, and the distribution of 40,000 - 50,000 tracts, of which apparently only three were found discarded.[22]

It has been asserted by some historians that religious objections were largely ineffectual in actually closing racecourses, but Burford was not the only example. Reading's site at King's Meadow passed into the hands of George Palmer, biscuit-maker, MP and a devout Quaker. The racing lease

---

[18] *RM* 18 Jan 1919

[19] HUGGINS. *Flat racing.* p207

[20] FOOTMAN. *History of the parish of St Michael and All Angels, Chipping Lambourn.* p149

[21] STAWELL. *History of Burford and Bibury racecourse.* p19

[22] OPEN AIR MISSION. *Races at Reading.*

expired in 1874, and was not renewed, the ground being required for more wholesome forms of public recreation. Stockbridge, where racing outlasted all its neighbouring courses, also fell victim to a landowner's disapproval, losing its lease in 1898.

Whilst the Jockey Club had not yet secured a full stranglehold on country racing (nor would it until the 1870s) there were emerging national criteria by which a race meeting might be judged to be keeping up with the times in the years 1830 - 1870: the number, length and type of the races; the professionalism of jockeys, trainers and race administration; the level of prize money, which determined the size and quality of fields. The only racecourse in Berkshire to keep pace with the changes was Ascot, which languished in the 1820s and 1830s, but was then rescued by investment, new management, the railway and Queen Victoria's somewhat dutiful patronage. When in 1861 the miseries of widowhood drove her from public life, Ascot soon found a new royal patron in her son Bertie, the Prince of Wales. Whilst his horses trained on the local downland, and he was fond of Stockbridge racecourse, royal patronage was not by and large exercised for the benefit of country racing.

In west Berkshire the tradition of races in heats lingered well into the 1850s, although by 1860 the switch had been made to five or six dash events per day. Reading, by 1858, was offering two days each with five dash events. Abingdon was a little slower to change. Both Abingdon and Reading continued throughout the nineteenth century to schedule races for hunters and galloways alongside thoroughbred contests, a combination which was thought to reflect poorly on the class of meeting. Hungerford demonstrated a strong attachment to pony races. Hurdles, abhorred by the Jockey Club, appeared on west Berkshire race cards, especially at East Ilsley in the 1850s. There were still matches between gentlemen riders, in which professional jockeys were handicapped with extra weight. Some meetings held races which were specifically limited to local horses and riders.[23] The pattern of entries sometimes reflected rather harder racing than would have been inflicted on valuable bloodstock; at Hungerford in 1869 a Mr Brown's horse *Darkie* ran at least three times in two days. However, although officially regarding such meetings as incompatible with the standards of modern Flat

---

[23] *RCs* various 1849-65

racing, the Jockey Club still calendared them, and even adjudicated disputes at East Ilsley, Hungerford and Abingdon.

Undoubtedly the changing social and economic climate was becoming hostile to old-style, local country racing. Ten courses within the Newbury 40-mile circle which had been active and calendared in the early years of the nineteenth century had expired by its mid-point: Maidenhead (1800); Burford (1802, although uncalendared racing continued until 1859); Newbury (1815); Chippenham (1816); Cricklade and Horndean (1818); Burderop (1831); Devizes (1838); Bicester (1841); Hurstbourne Tarrant (1846). Bucklebury's pony course probably also vanished at some time during this period. The 1850s culled two more: Basingstoke (1850) and East Ilsley (1858). The 1860s were, comparatively, less lethal. Only Hungerford retired from the calendar in this decade when, as will be seen in the next chapter, two seemingly defunct courses sprang unexpectedly back to life.

9

Winners and losers
The last of country racing and the birth of Newbury Racecourse

In 1865 the village of Lambourn still had no railway connection, nor indeed much in the way of modern communications. Just one road led south-east to Newbury, and another north-east to Wantage. Only two carriers were based in the village. It was scarcely a promising venue for a racing revival, but the second Earl of Craven nonetheless advertised a listed two-day meeting here, on Weathercock Down opposite his seat of Ashdown House. Only one race had £100 of added money; the rest were £30 to £50, and the card included hunter races, hurdles and a gentlemen's race won by that archaic figure, the owner-rider.[1] Entries were mostly in single figures per race. No record exists of the meeting's attendance, but there would have been scant accommodation other than for house guests of Ashdown, which was itself little more than a hunting lodge. This meeting looks more like an exercise in bravura sporting hospitality than an engagement with the modern racing scene. Any prospect of a repeat was pre-empted by the earl's death a year later.

Fig 21. Ashdown House, the Craven seat near Upper Lambourn. It now belongs to the National Trust.

---

[1] *RC 1865*

The following year however another revival took place at the opposite end of the county. Windsor Races reopened on a new course on Rays Island, surrounded by the Thames. Although the racecourse was heavily overshadowed by its mighty neighbour at Ascot, the town of Windsor, 22 miles from London and 19 miles from Reading, was blessed with two railways: a south-western branch line through Richmond and Staines to Waterloo, and the GWR to Paddington. The royal residence was close by, although royal racing favours were Ascot's prerogative, and Windsor could not hope to compete in this respect. Nonetheless the course was of a modern, commodious design by John Frail, and the meetings prospered sufficiently to ride the wave of Jockey Club regulation over the next 20 years. They continue to this day.

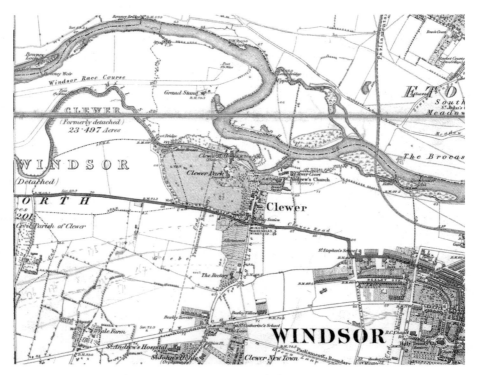

Fig 22. Windsor Racecourse (top left) mapped in the 1880s.

In 1870 the Jockey Club announced that henceforth no race meeting which was not run under Rules would be listed in the *Racing Calendar*. Thereafter such non-JC meetings came to be known as 'flapping meetings'. Reading and Abingdon were, at this point, west Berkshire's only active courses, and neither was wholly compliant with Rules. Both were in financial difficulty, and each had a particular problem; at Reading it was an unsympathetic landowner, and Abingdon was about to lose its apparently irreplaceable clerk. For these and no doubt other more general reasons, west Berkshire's two most enduring racecourses had finally closed by 1875.

Perhaps the news that west Berkshire no longer had calendared racing influenced the third Earl of Craven (1841 - 1883) in his decision to resume the Lambourn race series that had been so briefly re-ignited by his father in 1865. George Craven enjoyed a reputation for liberal hospitality to field sportsmen at his Ashdown seat where, in 1870, he had hosted the well attended Ashdown Diversions, the hunt meeting described in chapter six. In 1876 he launched Lambourn's last series, which combined the character of country racing with the new and ever more stringent Rules. Unlike the Ashdown Diversions these meetings were listed in the *Racing Calendar*.

However George Craven was no Turfite, and it is likely that the inspiration for these meetings originated with Lord Rosebery, the future prime minister, and the (first) Duke of Westminster, the richest man in England. They were two of the most prominent racing men of the era, and they had horses in training at Russley Park. In the late 1870s they rented Ashdown House for its proximity to these stables (within gunshot, as the *Newbury Weekly News* put it).[2] The Craven family (and fox-hounds) had moved temporarily to more convenient accommodation further west.

Whichever was the begetter, the first Lambourn meeting of this series in 1876 was relatively low-key, with Lord Craven and Lord Rosebery the most high-profile attenders. Seven races filled the one-day card, each with either £50 or £100 of added money. The following year the meeting, upped to two days, advertised itself as under Jockey Club Rules, and with no fewer than 17 stewards, including lords Craven, Rosebery and Kesteven. Berkshire gentry turned out *en masse*. Some famous professional jockeys took part, including Fred Archer, and the *Newbury Weekly News* correspondent had no doubt that this most celebrated jockey would have found the downland course pleasanter and more picturesque than many of the more famous venues to which he was accustomed.[3]

---

[2] *NWN* 13 Dec 1883
[3] *NWN* 26 Jul 1877

Fig. 23. Poster for Lambourn Races 1878.

However Lambourn's late flowering in the racing calendar expired with the third meeting in 1878, which had the misfortune of coinciding with an epidemic at Russley Park stables and bad weather. Entries were down, and the last race did not even fill. The newspaper report made no mention of distinguished Turfites present, despite a starry list of stewards on the poster advertising the event. Even Lord Craven did not attend, being absent on a deep-sea fishing trip with his family.[4]

The years of this Lambourn series encompassed a key event in the apotheosis of the Jockey Club. In January 1877 the club decreed that to comply with Rules all calendared race meetings must have £300 of added prize money per day, with races of a mile or more to be worth at least £150. To this was added the following year a minimum prize money requirement of £100 for every race.[5] This target far exceeded the subscription prospects of most country courses, where £100 might be offered for the best one or two races, but £50 for the rest.

In addition to this burden, another landmark development in the sport spelt doom for country racecourses. In 1875 the first enclosed course was opened at Sandown Park, where racegoers queued at a turnstile to pay half-a-crown entrance fee. The following year Kempton Park was founded on the same principle, and enclosure was then rapidly and widely adopted. A much earlier experiment in London had foundered on rights of way, which rendered charging for access illegal, but soon after 1875, at almost every course not situated on common land, gate-money was revolutionising finances, marginalising such old-style, aristocratic patronage as remained. In return, organisers were under pressure to supply the kind of racing experience demanded by the paying public. This meant investment in safety, security, accommodation and the track itself, not to mention keen competition to attract the best horses. With the possibility of excluding undesirables, enclosed racecourses improved their image, and even wooed women racegoers with exclusive facilities. The demands of the market were matched by those of the Jockey Club, which in 1883 introduced licensing for racecourses, together with new and obligatory standards of provision. Heavy investment would henceforth be necessary and, to obtain a satisfactory return on this, several meetings a year became necessary, far more than could be sustained by purely local support. The transition of racing from a local to a national sport, begun by the railways, was now complete.

---

[4] *NWN* 4 Jul 1878
[5] HUGGINS. *Flat racing*. p183

The 1878 meeting at Lambourn was west Berkshire's last listed race for nearly 30 years. Oxford's Port Meadow, on common land, could neither improve nor enclose, and racing in Oxfordshire ended for good in 1880. In the next few years Hampshire's stragglers succumbed: Southampton in 1881, Winchester in 1887, Portsmouth in 1894. Stockbridge, where the patronage of the Prince of Wales had attracted some alluring prize money, retained its fashionable and successful status until 1898, when a change of landownership resulted in withdrawal of the racecourse lease. By then there was scant incentive to look for a new site. After Marlborough's demise in 1874 Wiltshire was represented in the *Racing Calendar* only by Salisbury.

By recognizing only thoroughbred Flat racing and, through the NHC, steeplechasing, the Jockey Club created an unbridgeable divide between this now highly regulated national sport and the remnants of informal local racing. As the club regulations of the 1870s and 80s took hold, cross-over events of the kind which had flourished in Lambourn, Hungerford and Ilsley became impossible. Professional jockeys and thoroughbreds taking part alongside hunters and ponies now risked a total ban from mainstream racing. Hunt races went their own way, as has been described in chapter six, leaving the more robust forms of popular racing as a part of traditional folk festivals, but these too were being sanitised by the militant respectability of the Victorian middle classes. The drunken rowdiness of rustic fairs was deplored, such that the pony-racing of the Chapel Row Revels (once thought to be a civilized alternative to cudgel-fighting) had by 1895 been replaced by a merry-go-round of wooden horses bearing the names of Classic winners.[6]

The Scouring of the White Horse was also cleansed of riotous pleasures. In 1780 the three-day revels had included a cart-horse race in full harness (crossing and jostling allowed), a tobacco-smoking contest for Gypsy women (first prize a gallon of gin), cudgel-fighting for a gold-laced hat, wrestling for a pair of silver buckles, and a hazardous dash after a huge cheese rolled down the Manger, which was a steep dip beside White Horse Hill. (A witness related that the runners included a 'sweep chimley' and a 'millud', and that the latter tripped up the former.[7]) But in the next century attitudes were changing, and the 1857 games had a bad year. The cart-horse race resulted in a human fatality, and the pig-chase degenerated into a violent dispute between five claimants, none of whom gained the prize because it had died in the *fraças*. Furthermore, thieves broke into some of

---

[6] NWN 23 Sep 1895 *Chit Chat*
[7] *VCH Berks* vol ii p314

the booths and stole takings. These games were 'long and fondly remembered' by some,[8] but such mayhem was no longer acceptable. By 1876 the ritual had been neutered into a more seemly picnic with croquet and visits to sites of historical interest. By the end of the century the work of scouring the chalk figure, for centuries carried out by local villagers, was undertaken privately by the Countess of Craven, wholly unaccompanied by local participation.

These more idiosyncratic, localised revels were replaced by national celebrations centred on the new bank holidays, royal weddings and jubilees. They were more regulated proceedings, but they often included informal horse-racing. Newbury's celebrations for the royal marriage of March 1871, organised under the wholesome label of Rural Sports and Gymnastic Exercises, featured pony and hurdle races from which Lambourn's stable lads were expressly banned. Rural sports were usually town-centred; the organizers were messrs. Plenty, Wheeler, Jackson, and Ryott, names representative of Newbury's urban business élite.[9] Hungerford's Easter Monday Rural Sports of 1881 featured the Hungerford Grand National Steeplechase over a flagged course across Port Down and the river meadows. The prize was £3. The same event in 1890 had several pony and galloway races, for which the two biggest prizes (£15 and £25) bore the names of Craven and Hungerford Park, but it is not clear if this indicated gentry sponsorship.[10] Horse-racing was clearly the major event of the Newbury Rural Sports of Easter Monday 1894, in which three races (one of hurdles) were run in heats for five, seven and 15 guineas. There was no professional betting, and thoroughbreds were to carry an extra 14 pounds.[11] Such races were gradually dropped from Newbury's rural sports early in the twentieth century, possibly because of the limitations of the ground – one circuit of Newbury's Marsh was a bare six furlongs. Hungerford had the benefit of more space on the common, and bank holiday pony-racing survived here into the 1930s. Pony-racing was a particular *bête-noire* of the Jockey Club although, with the support of the Earl of Carnarvon, it was finally recognized through the creation of the Pony Turf Club in 1926.

Newbury's more serious racegoers, not to mention the area's estimated 1,500 horses in training, had to travel some distance for racing under Rules. Towards the end of the nineteenth century the nearest tracks were Ascot Racecourse, going from strength to strength, Windsor

---

[8] WILLIAMS. *Villages of the White Horse.* p274
[9] *NWN* 16 Mar 1871
[10] *NWN* 27 Mar 1890
[11] *NWN* 17 Apr 1894

EASTER MONDAY.

HUNGERFORD
RURAL SPORTS.

THE following PRIZES to be competed for on the DOWNS, by kind permission of the High Constable, T. ALEXANDER, Esq.

Stewards :—T. Alexander, Esq. (High Constable), Messrs. J. Adnams, E. M. Allen, J. Booth, J. Cottrell, L. Cundell, Dr Major, J. Platt, jun., V. Parsloe, H. Richens, J. Walker, and J. Wooldridge.

Colonel WILLES, Judge.

TO COMMENCE AT ONE O'CLOCK.

Bicycle Race—Open; entry, 5s. each; about 4 miles on road. Four starters or no race. Winner, £5; second, £1; third, 5s.

Flat Race—Open; 100 yards; entry, 1s. each. Winner, £1; second, 5s.; third, 2s. 6d.

Flat Race—Open; one mile; entry, 1s. each. Winner, £2; second, 10s.; third, 5s.

Hurdle Race—Open; 220 yards; entry, 1s. each; over 8 flights of hurdles. Winner, £1; second, 7s. 6d.; third, 2s. 6d.

Sack Race—Open; entry, 6d. each; 60 yards. Winner, 7s. 6d.; second, 2s. 6d.; third, 1s.

High Jump—Open; entry, 1s. each. Winner, 7s. 6d.: second, 2s. 6d.

Long Jump—Open; entry, 1s. each. Winner, 7s. 6d.; second, 2s. 6d.

Flat Race—150 yards; for residents in the parish of Hungerford; entry, 1s. each. Winner, 10s.; second, 5s.; third, 2s. 6d.

Flat Race—One mile; for residents in the parish of Hungerford; entry, 1s. each. Winner, £1; second, 10s.; third, 5s.; fourth, 2s. 6d.

Hungerford Grand National Steeple-Chase —No entrance fee—from Newbury-road, across the meadows, Kennett and Dunn Rivers, and Canal, to the winning post on the Downs, over the course flagged out. Winner, £3; second, £1 10s.; third, 10s.; fourth, 5s.; fifth, 2s. 6d. Entries to be given in at the Stewards' tent before four o'clock.

Donkey Race—½ mile; open; catch weights; entry, 1s. each. Winner, £1; second, 10s.

Pony Race—about ½ mile; not over 12½ hands; catch weights; entry, 5s. each. Four starters or no race. Winner, £3; second, £1.

Pony Race—about ½ mile; not over 13½ hands; catch weights; entry, 5s. each. Four starters or no race. Winner, £3; second, £1.

Galloway Race—one mile; not over 14-2 hands; weight, 10 stone; over six flights of hurdles. Four starters or no race. Winner, £5; second, £1.

Jumping Prize—for Horses. Jumping the only point of merit. Weight, 12 stone. Entry, 10s. Cup, value £5 5s.

Tug of War—four teams. Winners, £1; second, 10s. Nominated by the Stewards.

All Races to close on Wednesday, April 13th, 1881, at 8 p.m., at the Three Swans Hotel, at which time all entries to be paid and colours declared.

All Ponies and Galloways to be measured at the Three Swans Hotel before 12 o'clock.

The Stewards reserve to themselves the right of refusing any entry. The decision of the Judge to be final.

A BAND will be in attendance.

H. J. BEARD,
Secretary and Treasurer.

Hungerford, March 12th, 1881.

Fig 24. Advertisement for Hungerford's Rural Sports of 1881.

Racecourse, never in the front rank but steadily popular, and Salisbury Racecourse, the stayer which had scarcely missed a year certainly since 1727 and probably much earlier. The Jockey Club's licensing of racecourses, introduced in 1883, was designed to cap numbers and maintain quality. The club was disinclined to acknowledge the anomaly that the racecourse map of England had a black hole in the training heartland of the central south.

The obvious site for a modern racecourse was Newbury, which was the urban centre of the downland training area that spanned three counties: Berkshire, eastern Wiltshire and north Hampshire. Newbury had a substantial population base and was, by the late nineteenth century, well placed in the railway network with links east-west and north-south. In addition, the Lambourn Valley Railway opened in 1898, linking the village with Newbury. No longer did Lambourn-trained horses have to walk 10 miles to Uffington station on the main GWR line. The possibility of a racecourse was under local discussion in the 1890s, as an idea originally credited to the Duke of Westminster (who had, on the retirement of Robert Peck at Russley Park, moved his horses to John Porter's Kingsclere yard of Park House, and later took a financial interest in the establishment). The flat farmland of Greenham Lodge Estate had already been identified as a suitable site. Lloyd Harry Baxendale, the landowner, was actively interested in the idea, and by the end of 1897 a course had even been provisionally marked out between the foot of the St Mary's Church hill and Pigeons Farm.

Fig 25. Greenham mapped in the 1880s. This Ordnance Survey map shows the site on which Newbury Racecourse was to be developed in 1905.

Local opinion was not unanimously in favour, however. A petition against the proposed Newbury racecourse was raised on grounds of detriment to local trade and public life as well, of course, as the undesirability of promoting gambling. With 600 signatures representing the town's traders and clergy, this was forwarded to Lloyd Baxendale, who summarily dismissed it in the columns of the *Newbury Weekly News*. The signatories, he said, were ignorant of the subject, and their protest would therefore not influence him.[12] Something, however, did discourage him

Fig 24. John Porter, trainer of Kingsclere and founder of Newbury Racecourse.

(probably the intransigence of the Jockey Club) and the idea appears to have been dropped. When it resurfaced five years later (the first Duke of Westminster was by this time dead) the instigator was John Porter, who frequently recounted a story of travelling eastwards out of Newbury by train, and speculating on the suitability of the Greenham Lodge estate for a racecourse.

Lloyd Baxendale was still interested, and an option to purchase land was negotiated in late 1903. However John Porter's application for a Newbury racecourse licence met with no enthusiasm from the Jockey Club.[13] The story of Porter's meeting with Edward VII (for whom he had trained as Prince of Wales) as he left the club's Newmarket offices has entered local legend. The king enquired as to Porter's business and, on hearing of the project, asked to see the plans. Royal influence was subsequently exerted on the club committee, and the application was approved.[14] In part the granting of the application was justified by the recent failure of Northampton Racecourse, which allowed Newbury to be licensed with no overall increase in the number of racecourses.

---

[12] *NWN* 2 & 9 Dec 1897
[13] PORTER. *John Porter of Kingsclere.* p444
[14] OSGOOD. *Story of Newbury racecourse.* p1-2

The first meeting of the newly-formed Newbury Racecourse Company was held in late August 1904. Shares were taken up by the second Duke of Westminster, Lord Howard de Walden, the banker Ernest Cassel, (all clients of Park House stables) J. Musker, James Buchanan (a distiller) and Lloyd Baxendale. The board of directors comprised Lloyd Baxendale, John Porter, James Buchanan and Oscar Rayner, a barrister and racehorse owner who lived at Chieveley Manor. George Gardner Leader, the solicitor whose firm still exists in Newbury, was appointed secretary and solicitor to the new company.[15] At this time John Porter was still training at Park House, and had recently bought Strattons, where he set up a stud. On being appointed managing director of the racecourse in 1905 he retired from Park House, sold Strattons, and built Ormonde House for himself in Newbury. (Ormonde House later became Newbury College, but was razed at the end of the twentieth century for redevelopment.)

Fig 27. Members of the Newbury Racecourse Company on the steps of the grandstand. W. E. Busby (clerk), G. Gardner Leader (secretary), C. W. Stephens (architect), O. W. Rayner, J. Porter and L. Baxendale (directors).

---

[15] *NWN* passim 1904-05 and OSGOOD. *Story of Newbury racecourse*

Negotiations were also under way with the GWR for a station at the racecourse. This was more necessity than novelty, as some 30 of the country's racecourses already had their own stations.[16] The GWR's initial demand for £5,000 from the racecourse company was refused, and eventually the parties settled upon £2,000 and £160 for each of the next three years, to be continued if the GWR's receipts from the investment fell below £1,500 a year. There were protracted negotiations not only over financing, but also land occupancy, station accommodation, access, train services, fares, unboxing facilities for racehorses and the fate of existing level crossings. Just two months before the first meeting a whole new plan was drawn up. Nonetheless, the station was ready on time, and racegoers could travel from London in less than an hour for ten shillings first class, or two-and-six for third class.[17]

Fig. 28. Newbury racecourse grandstand prior to opening day. The circular feature on the left is the royal box.

The course was left-handed track, 105-feet wide, and two miles round a figure nine. An early commentator, F. H. Bayles, observed that the finish constituted 'a very dead and trying gallop calculated to distress horses after a hard race'. Nonetheless he praised the water hydrants and the 105 well-

---

[16] TOLSON & VAMPLEW. 'Derailed: railways and horse racing revisited.' *Sports Historian* 18 (2) Nov 98 pp34-50
[17] West Berkshire Museum. Bundle 2004.7 Racecourse

ventilated loose-boxes, with boys' mess rooms and dormitories near the stabling. The jockeys' hospital with two doctors and a nurse present at all meetings was another noteworthy feature, by no means standard at all racecourses. For the horses there was a veterinary surgeon and horse ambulance.[18]

As opening day approached it was clear that some opinion-formers in Newbury were antagonistic. The *Newbury Weekly News* was edited by a devout Primitive Methodist who, whilst dutifully reporting news about racecourse progress, gave it little encouragement and appears to have accepted no advertisement for the inaugural meeting. In a leader the week before he expressed grave doubts about what the racecourse would bring to Newbury, deploring that racegoers seemed unable to derive pleasure from the pure sport itself, and must stoop to gambling. His message was reinforced from the town's pulpits the Sunday before race week. In the town's principal church of St Nicolas, the Rev. Lionel Majendie preached a sermon on the evils of betting, concluding with an exhortation to his congregation to stay away from the new racecourse. Similar sermons were delivered in the dissenting chapels, the Methodists deploring in particular that a course inspection had taken place on the Sabbath.[19]

Heavy rain preceded the inaugural meeting of Tuesday 26th and Wednesday 27th September 1905, and did not let up for the full two days. (Jane Austen would no doubt have seen some significance in this.) Nonetheless an estimated 15,000 passed through the turnstiles. A continuous succession of motor cars was reported through the centre of Newbury all morning, as well as a substantial number of carriages. The latter (provided that their occupants were members) could park without charge in a designated enclosure on the course, but motor vehicles paid two-and-six (or five shillings under cover). Six thousand racegoers arrived by rail at the new station, to which the GWR ran race-day specials from London, Oxford, Cheltenham, Swindon, Cardiff, Bristol, Southampton, Dudley, Wolverhampton and Sheffield.

The members' enclosure (400 people had taken out annual subscriptions of seven guineas) held an estimated 3,000 to 4,000, who could take shelter in the grandstand or even, for £10 - £20 extra, in a private box. All of these had been booked well in advance, because many of the big houses of the district were holding house parties for the occasion. To the disappointment of the organizers, Edward VII was not present to grace the

---

[18] BAYLES. *Race courses atlas of Great Britain and Ireland.*

[19] *NWN* 21 & 28 Sep 1905

royal box, as had at one time been hoped for. Newbury was to wait another two years for this honour.

Entry to Tattersalls next door, with a smaller stand, cost £1. Lowliest of all, the Cheap Enclosure offered no protection from the rain, but even so, 9,443 racegoers paid two shillings and sixpence to enter. A group of non-payers stationed themselves on the new road leading down the hill from Greenham Church, from where they got a distant view of the course, but no very clear idea of what was going on.

The races themselves were equally well supported. Six stewards (five of them titled) officiated, and 98 horses were saddled for the first day's six races. The big one was the Inaugural Handicap, with a first prize of £1,600, which was won by Lord Carnarvon's horse *Missovaja*. Other races had first prizes of between £150 and £400. The second day, attended by 7,764, scheduled six races with a similar spread of prize money, but with a top race of £1,000. Moët & Chandon had applied to add 50 cases of wine to one race prize, but this early bid for commercial sponsorship was not permitted.[20]

Security was a major concern for a modern racecourse anxious to distance itself from the sport's traditionally rough image, and there was the additional burden of traffic management. The chief constable of Berkshire Constabulary was present, but it was not clear whether he was on duty or enjoying the social occasion.[21] Around the course there were 134 uniformed men, augmented by some plain-clothes detectives mingling with the crowd. By and large the day went smoothly, although three pickpockets were arrested. Whilst held in the cells their fingerprints were dispatched to Scotland Yard, which returned the information that they were regular offenders. This was an early and much applauded use of the new forensic science.[22] Bookies were much in evidence, but no doubt in compliance with the current law, which forbade them to occupy fixed premises on the course.

The sporting press greeted this meeting with a torrent of unqualified praise, although one should perhaps allow for the deferential style of Edwardian journalism, especially in matters dominated by the ruling class. Newbury Racecourse's list of credits, from shareholders through directors and patrons down to stewards, attested to the vigorous survival of the nobility in racing. Prominent in these ranks was the Herbert family (earls of Carnarvon), whose Highclere estate had hosted the Newbury/Woodhay

---

[20] OSGOOD. *Story of Newbury racecourse.* p4
[21] *NWN* 28 Sep 1905 p8
[22] *NWN* 5 Oct 1905 p8

races of 1812 - 1815. Although more commonly remembered for his Egyptian exploits, George Herbert, the fifth Earl of Carnarvon (1866 - 1923), served as a Newbury Racecourse steward and was also a founder member of the Thoroughbred Breeders Association. His son Henry Herbert, the sixth earl (1898 - 1987), was another noted owner-breeder, as well as a successful amateur rider of the 1930s. The seventh earl (1924 - 2001) became racing manager to Queen Elizabeth II. All three were closely involved with Newbury Racecourse.

The commercial benefits to Newbury were considerable, notwithstanding the fears of the 1897 petitioners, who had claimed that a local racecourse would be a net disadvantage to the town's economy. Contracts were awarded to several Newbury companies, such as Stradling and Plenty, a bicycle and auto dealer who secured the car parking and repair concession. Given the unreliability of early motor cars this was probably quite lucrative. Joseph Hopson, a Newbury furniture retailer whose business lives on today as Camp Hopson, supplied an invalid couch which is still in the royal box. For dealing with more serious casualties Newbury Hospital was allocated £5 a year. The catering contract went to a London company, Bertram & Co, no doubt to the chagrin of Newbury victuallers. A few diversifications were deemed unsuitable; proposals for golf and aviation facilities were rejected by the racecourse management, at least in Edwardian years.[23]

Quite a few racegoers used the occasion to visit the town itself, and in later years visits to Newbury Races became associated with the opportunity to stock up on local specialities such as sausages and lardy cakes.

The Jockey Club licensed Newbury Racecourse for three meetings the following year, soon increased to seven. A steeplechase course was constructed in 1906, its 12 fences 'built to regulation order, and devilish well too!' according to F. H. Bayles.[24] Newbury Races had clearly come to stay. Local opposition quickly fell silent. Indeed, following the first race meeting, the deputy editor of the *Newbury Weekly News*, a man of more flexible views than his boss, dared to opine in his *Chit-Chat* column that, despite the doom-mongering, nothing dreadful had happened; Newbury's streets were a little more lively, the hotels more prosperous. He marvelled at the count of 78 cars passing over Newbury Bridge in one hour. However the story of Newbury Racecourse and the motor car belongs to the next eight decades.

---

[23] OSGOOD. *Story of Newbury racecourse.* p5-12
[24] BAYLES. *Race courses atlas of Great Britain and Ireland.*

Appendix 1 The Cravens in racing

life dates	name, relation, title	residence & racing activities
1702-64	**Fulwar**, brother of 3rd baron, became **4th baron** 1739	lived at Hamstead Marshall and Ashdown; racehorse breeder and owner; founded courses and subscribed prizes at Lambourn and Wantage; founded Craven Hunt; Jockey Club member and subscriber to Cheny's listing 1726, 1736
1705-69	**William**, cousin of 4th baron, became **5th baron** 1764	racehorse owner; continued support of racing at Lambourn; regular steward at Abingdon; MFH Craven Hunt; Jockey Club member
1738-91	**William**, nephew of 5th baron, became **6th baron** 1769	lived at Benham Valence; racehorse breeder and owner; steward and supporter of racing at Lambourn, Wantage, Abingdon, Andover; founded Craven meeting at Newmarket 1771; Jockey Club member
1750-1828	**Elizabeth**, wife of 1) 6th baron 1766; 2) **Margrave** of Anspach 1791	lived at Benham Valence; racehorse owner, as was her second husband the Margrave; supported Enborne meetings
1771-1825	**William**, son of 6th baron, became **7th baron** 1791 and **1st earl 1801**	lived at Ashdown; racehorse owner; member of Jockey Club; steward at Abingdon; continued support of racing at Lambourn until enclosure 1803; founded racing at Newbury/Enborne 1805-1811
1776-1836	**Henry Augustus Berkeley**, son of 6th baron	heavy gambler; shot himself because of losses incurred 1836 Derby
1779-1851	**Richard Keppel**, 3rd son of 6th baron	lived at Benham Valence 1799 until sold it to Frederick Villebois; steward at Newbury/Enborne/Woodhay 1805-15
1782-1860	**Fulwar**, son of John Craven	lived at Beckhampton; racehorse owner and eccentric; steward at Burderop 1825
1809-66	**William**, son of 1st earl, became **2nd earl** 1825	lived at Ashdown; owner of *Charity* (Grand National winnner 1841) co-owner of *Wild Dayrell* (Derby winner 1855); steward Newbury steeplechase 1841; revived the Lambourn meeting 1865
	Frederick, brother of 2nd earl	racehorse-owner
1841-83	**George Grimston**, 2nd son of 2nd earl, became **3rd earl** 1866	lived at Ashdown; hosted Ashdown Diversions (hunt races) of 1870; revived Lambourn Flat meetings 1876-78; MFH Old Berks Hunt
1843-	**Osbert William**, 3rd son of 2nd earl	lived at Ashdown; steward at Lambourn meetings 1876-78; MFH Old Berks Hunt
1835-1906	**William George**, eldest son of George Augustus Craven who was 2nd son of 1st earl	jockey and owner of Flat horses and steeplechasers; Jockey Club member/steward and prominent writer on racing; active promoter of steeplechasing and co-founder of National Hunt Committee 1866

Appendix 2 Racecourses within 40 miles of Newbury and their approximate years of operation

		pre1700	1700-40	1741-74	1775-99	1800-24	1825-49	1850-74	1875-99	1900+
Berks	Abingdon		1730 - 31	1767				1875		
	Ascot		1711							present day
	Bucklebury					1822	1850?			
	East Ilsley		1727=36			1804		1849 =58		
	Faringdon		1740							
	Hungerford							1859 =69		
	Lambourn		1731=40	1749		1803	1840 =49	1865	1876 =78	
	Maidenhead		1728		1800					
	Newbury		1738=40			1805 =15				1905 →
	Reading		1727			1813		1843 =74		
	Wantage		1727 - 28		1793 =96					
	Windsor/Datchet	1684		1741=45	1780					
Oxon	Banbury		1720 = 39				1830 = 1846			
	Bicester	1685	1716 = 37				1837 =41			
	Burford	1620 1681		1743		1802				
	Chipping Norton		1734 ----- 1757							
	Goring		1728 --32							
	Henley		1732 --39							
	Oxford	1630+	1727				1842. 1848 - 49.	1859 = 1880		present day
	Woodstock		1733							

		pre1700	1700-40	1741-74	1775-99	1800-24	1825-49	1850-74	1875-99	1900+
Wilts	Burderop		1740			1811------1831				
	Chippenham			1741		1808---16				
	Cricklade					1814---18				
	Devizes						1835---38			
	Marlborough		1730------	------------	------------	----1811	1840 --------	----1874		
	Salisbury	1585+	1727 ══════	══════	══════	══════	══════	══════	══════	present day
Hants	Alton		1740							
	Andover			1759--------	----1775					
	Basingstoke		1737---	------------	------------	------------	----1850			
	Corhampton							1871		
	Gosport				1787					
	Horndean					1818				
	Hurstbourne Tarrant						1846			
	Lyndhurst							1859 - 71		
	Odiham			1760--------	------------	------------	------------	------------	----1879	
	Portsmouth					1819	1845-46		1891-94	
	Southampton					1804---	------------	------------	----1881	
	Stockbridge		1737 ══════	══════	══════	══════	══════	══════	1898	
	Winchester		1740------	------------	------------	------------	------------	------------	----1887	
	Winton			1741						

calendared Flat meetings

probable/uncalendared meetings

═══ indicates continuous series

--- indicates intermittent series

113

Appendix 3 Site descriptions of racecourses in Berkshire 1700-1905

location	approx dates	site	course description
Abingdon	1730-1811	Culham Heath	south of Abingdon, across the border in Oxon
	1812-1875	Abingdon Commons	common land west of Abingdon; 1.25 miles, flat oval; grandstand; marked on OS 6" series
	1875-1900	Otney Meadows (s/chase)	beside the River Ock, towards Sutton
Ascot	1711-today	Ascot Heath	Crown land to north west of town; protected for racing by law; 66yards short of 2 miles in 1857; shown on OS 6"series
Bucklebury	18thC? - 1850?	Chapel Row Common	pony racecourse associated with Revels; a bisected oval measuring 1,353 yards around, and 968 yards up the middle; exact period of operation unknown, but flourishing in 1820s
East Ilsley	1727-1858	Kates' Gore on Prestall Down	2 miles north of East Ilsley on Newbury-Oxford road (A34) at foot of Gore Hill; Grim's Ditch passes through site; Kates Gore marked on John Rocque map of 1761 and OS 6" series, but not Prestall Down; names not in use today
Faringdon	1740		nothing known of exact site; almost certainly on Craven land
Hungerford	1840-69	Port Down	common land to east of town, near station; course more than 1 mile round, marked out each year with temporary grandstand; irregularity of ground made results difficult to forecast; when calendared racing ceased non-thoroughbred racing continued on same ground
Lambourn	1731-1803	Row Down	downland west of Upper Lambourn owned by Lord Craven; course shaped as a figure 9, with a straight side of rather over a mile, and a rise and fall throughout; marked on John Rocque map of 1761; probably enclosed 1804; now gallops
	1865, 1870s	Weathercock Down	downland owned by Lord Craven opposite Ashdown House; now gallops
Maidenhead	1728-1800	Maidenhead Thicket	

location	approx dates	site	course description
Newbury	1738-77	Wash Common	common land to south of Newbury, owned by corporation; enclosed 1850s; now built over
	1805-11	Enborne Heath	common land owned by Lord Craven; 1 mile west of Newbury; enclosed 1811 and converted to Crockham Heath Farm; still mostly farmland, opposite Enborne School
	1812-15	East Woodhay Heath (Hants)	common land owned by Lord Carnarvon; 2 miles south-west of Newbury; probably enclosed 1815+
	1815	Northcroft	common land on west side of town, used for non-thoroughbred racing on 2nd week of 1805-15 meetings, also for hurdles after steeplechases; still a public green space/recreation ground
	1839	Sydmonton (s/chase)	3.5-mile course from Sydmonton to Ecchinswell (formerly Itchingswell) over River Enborne. Watership Down nearby is also locally reputed to be an 'old racecourse'
	1840-41	Enborne (s/chase)	farmland between River Enborne and Skinners Green/Enborne Gate, 1 mile west of Newbury; some houses in Enborne Row described in 1881 census as at 'old racecourse'; still farmland but bisected by Newbury bypass
	late 19thC	Marsh	town-centre recreation ground used for rural sports including non-thoroughbred racing; now called Victoria Park and still a public green space/recreation ground
	1905-today	Greenham	former Baxendale estate land east-south-east of Newbury; own railway station
Reading	1727-1814	various sites, settling upon Bulmersh Heath	common land east of town, owned by Blagraves; sold to Wheble who enclosed it 1814; course had 'a safe and convenient place for those on foot to see the sport' and a grandstand; now wholly built over

Appendix 3 Site descriptions of racecourses in Berkshire 1700-1905

location	approx dates	site	course description
Reading	1843-74	Kings Meadow	next to Thames, and close to town centre, bisected by river and railway; site owned first by Tompkins, later by Palmer family; course 70 yards short of 2 miles, flat, in a rough figure 9 with a straight run of 5 furlongs; several grandstands; landowner Palmer withdrew racing lease and dedicated land to more wholesome public recreation; fragment of public park still exists
	1857-80s	Chinnock's Farm (s/chase)	laid-out course with grandstand
	1890s-1939	Maiden Erleigh (s/chase)	South Berks Hunt and Yeomanry meetings
	1887-1939	Redstone Farm at Hawthorn Hill (s/chase)	used principally for hunt & military steeplechases
Wantage	1727-96	Letcombe Regis	downland owned by Lord Craven; exact location unknown
Windsor/	17thC, 1740s,		Henry VIII raced at Datchet Mead and in Windsor Great Park; Charles II raced at Datchet Ferry;
Datchet	1866-today	Rays Island, Clewer	modern course established 1866 at Rays Island on the Thames, above Clewer; shown on OS 6" series.

Bibliography of sources cited in footnotes

References and abbreviations

Sources are identified as footnotes at the bottom of each page, giving author surname, title and page numbers. This should be enough to identify the source in the bibliography, which gives full reference details. Some frequently quoted titles have been abbreviated in the footnotes as follows

JOJ	*Jackson's Oxford Journal*
NWN	*Newbury Weekly News*
RC	*Racing Calendar 1773 -*
RM	*Reading Mercury 1725 -*
VCH Berks	*Victoria County History Berkshire*
VCH Hants	*Victoria County History Hampshire*
VCH Oxon	*Victoria County History Oxfordshire*
VCH Wilts	*Victoria County History Wiltshire*

1851 census Mach: Berkshire. CDROM Berkshire Family History Society (2003)

1881 British census and national index. CDROM The Church of Jesus Christ and Latter Day Saints.

ABINGDON Willoughby Bertie 4th earl of. *Adieu to the Turf.* (1778)

AESOP. *Sporting reminiscences in Hampshire.* Chapman & Hall. (1864)

Baily's turf guide

BARRETT Norman. *Daily Telegraph chronicle of horse racing.* Guinness. (1995)

BAYLES F. H. *Race courses atlas of Great Britain and Ireland.* (1903 and a later, undated edition)

Bensons British Turf register for 1855. Newcastle-upon-Tyne (1855-56)

Berkshire Chronicle 1825-

Bibliotheca topographica Britannica. John Nichols. (1780-90)

Billings directory and gazetteer for Berks & Oxon 1854

BLACK Robert. *Horse-racing in England.* (1893)

BLAINE Delabere Pritchett. *Encyclopaedia of rural sports.* (1840)

BOYD David. *Biographical dictionary of racehorse trainers.* privately published. (1998)

BOYD David. *Running horses.* privately published. (1978)

BOYD David. 'Sport of kings and queens.' *Berkshire Family Historian* (June 2002) p220-24

BROADLEY A. M. & MELVILLE L. *Beautiful Lady Craven.* Bodley. (1914)

BROWN Jonathan. *English market town.* Crowood. (1986)

BROWN-GRANT Evelyn. 'Banbury horse races.' *Cake and Cock Horse* v10, nos 2 & 3 (Spring & Summer 1986) pp26-31, 68-79

BYNG John. *Rides around Britain.* Folio Society. (1966)

CANNADINE David. *Decline and fall of the British aristocracy.* Papermac. (1996)

CHALLENOR Bromley ed. *Selections from the municipal chronicles of the borough of Abingdon 1555-1897.* Hooke. Abingdon (1898)

CHAPMAN R. W. ed. *Jane Austen's letters.* 2nd ed. OUP. (1952)

CHENY John. *Historical List of all horse-matches run, and of all plates and prizes run for in England.* (1727-1750)

CLOSE Francis Rev. *Evil consequences of attending the racecourse exposed in a sermon.* 3rd ed. Cheltenham (1827)

COBBETT William. *Rural ride.s* eds G. & M. Cole. Peter Davis. (1930) vol 1

COLE Benjamin. Map of Port Meadow. Oxford (1808)

COLE G & POSTGATE R. *Common people 1746-1946.* Methuen. (1948)

COOKE C. *Topographical and statistical description of the county of Berks.* (1805)

CORDEAUX E. H. & MERRY D. H. 'Port Meadow races.' *Oxoniensa* vxiii (1948) p55-65

CORNISH James. *Reminiscences of country life.* Country Life. (1939)

COX Mieneke. *Story of Abingdon pt VI: eighteenth-century county town.* privately published. (1989-1999)

CRAVEN Rupert (1870-1959). unpublished family memoir held in Reading University Library. Archive of Craven family papers. BER 27/14

DALBY L. J. *Wilts and Berks canal.* Oakwood Press. (c1986)

Dictionary of national biography. Concise ed. OUP. (1995)

DILS Joan ed. *Historical atlas of Berkshire.* Berkshire Record Society. Reading (1998)

DOUGLAS-HOME James. *Horse racing in Berkshire.* Sutton. Stroud (1992)

EADIE Emma Claire. *Structure and organisation of English horseracing 1830-1860.* University of Oxford thesis. (1993)

ESCOTT Thomas. *England its people polity & pursuits.* Chapman & Hall. (1877)

FILBY Michael. *Sociology of horse racing in Britain.* University of Warwick thesis. (1983)

FOOTMAN John. *History of the parish of St Michael and All Angels, Chipping Lambourn.* Eliot Stock. (1894)

FOWLER J. K. *Echoes of old country life* [Bucks]. Edward Arnold. (1892)

Gentleman's Magazine

GODWIN Henry. *Worthies and celebrities connected with Newbury and its neighbourhood.* Blacket. Newbury (1859)

GOLBY J. M. & PURDUE A. W. *Civilisation of the crowd; popular culture in England 1750-1900.* Sutton. Stroud (1999)

GRAY Edward. *History and antiquities of Newbury and its environs.* Chapman Hall. Speenhamland (1843)

GREAVES R. *Short history of the South Berks Hunt.* Reid Hamilton. (c1920)

GREAVES R. *Short history of the Vale of White Horse Hunt.* Reid Hamilton. (c1920)

Guide to the turf (1863)

HAMMOND Nigel. *Rural leisure in the Vale of the White Horse.* William Smith. Reading (1974)

HARRISON Brian. 'Animals and the state in nineteenth-century England.' *English Historical Review,* v88, issue 349 (Oct 1973) pp786-820

HARVEY Adrian. *Evolution of modern British sporting culture 1793-1850.* University of Oxford thesis. (1995)

HAZLITT William. *Selected essays* ed by George Sampson: The fight. CUP. (1971)

HEWETT William John. *History and antiquities of the hundred of Compton in Berks.* Snare. Reading (1844)

Horse racing: its history and early records of the principal and other race meetings. London (1863)

HOOKE W. H. *Abingdon, Berks.* (1924)

HOWITT William. *Rural life of England.* 2nd ed. Longmans, Green. (1840)

HUGGINS Mike. *Flat racing and British society a social and economic history 1790-1914.* Cass. (2000)

HUGGINS Mike. 'More sinful pleasures? Leisure respectability and the male middle classes in Victorian England.' *J of Social History* (Spring 2000)

HUGHES Thomas. *Scouring of the White Horse.* Macmillan. (1892)

HUMPHREYS Arthur. *Bucklebury: a Berkshire parish.* Reading (1932)

ITZKOWITZ D. 'Victorian bookmakers and their customers.' *Victorian Studies* v32 (1988) pp7-30

Jackson's Oxford Journal

KAY Joyce. 'Closing the stable door and the public purse: rise and fall of royal plates.' *Sports Historian* 20 (1) May 2000 pp18-29

KUTAPAN Michael. (catalogue of dead meetings) (c1985?) photocopy typescript in Cox Library

LA ROCHFOUCAULD François de. *Frenchman's year* [1784] *in Suffolk.* Suffolk Records Society. (1988)

LAWRENCE John. *History and delineation of the horse.* London (1809)

LEE Alan. *Cheltenham racecourse.* Pelham. (1985)

LENNOX William Pitt Lord. *Merrie England: its sports & pastimes.* T. C. Newby. (1858)

LEWIS Samuel. *Topographical dictionary of England.* (1840)

LODER-SYMONDS F. C. & CROWDY E. P. *History of the Old Berks Hunt 1760-1904.* Vinton. (1905)

LONGRIGG Roger. *Turf: three centuries of horse racing.* Eyre Methuen. (1975)

MAGEE Sean. *Ascot.* Sutton. Stroud (2000)

MALCOLMSON Robert. *Popular recreations in English society 1700-1850.* CUP. (1973)

MCGOWAN John. *Abingdon-Radley branch railway line.* privately published. (1982)

MCKIBBIN Ross. 'Working class gambling in Britain 1880-1930.' *Past & Present* v82 (1979) pp147-73

MCQUINN Tom. *Tales of the country eccentrics.* David & Charles. (1996)

MINGAY Gordon. *English landed society in 18th century.* Routledge Kegan Paul. (1963)

MINGAY Gordon. *Rural life in Victorian England.* Sutton. Stroud (1990)

MITCHELL Vic and SMITH Keith. *Slough to Newbury.* Middleton (2000)

MONEY Walter. *History of Newbury.* Oxford (1887)

MORTIMER Roger. *Biographical encyclopaedia of English flat racing.* Macdonald James. (1978)

MORTIMER Roger. *History of Derby Stakes.* Michael Joseph. (1973)

MORTIMER Roger. *Jockey Club.* Cassell. (1958)

MUNTING Roger. *Hedges and hurdles.* Allen. (1987)

Newbury Weekly News 1867-

News of a country town: extracts from Jacksons Oxford Journal 1753-1835 taken by James Townsend. OUP. (1914)

OPEN AIR MISSION. *Races at Reading* [statement] (1856) British Library. 4193.e.67.

NEWTON James. *Deserted village: diary of an Oxfordshire rector 1736-86.* ed Gavin Hannah. Sutton. Stroud (1992)

NICHOLS John. *Bibliotheca topographica Britannica* (Berkshire volume) (1780-90)

OAKSEY Robin. *Valley of the racehorse.* Headline. (2000)

OGILBY John. *Travellers' pocket book.* 23rd ed. Buckland Rivington. (1788)

ORDNANCE SURVEY maps 6" series Berkshire. 1867-81. CDROM Berkshire Family History Society and Berkshire Record Office

ORDNANCE SURVEY maps 25" series: Abingdon 1883; Stockbridge 1875; Oxford 1887; Reading 1883

OSBORNE Joseph. *Steeplechase and hurdle race epitome for season 1849-50.* Dublin (1850)

OSGOOD Frank. *Story of Newbury racecourse.* Kingsclere Publications. Newbury (1993)

PHILLIPS Daphne. *Great road to Bath.* Countryside Books. Newbury (1983)

PIGOT. *London & provincial new commercial directory Berks & Oxon* 1823 & 1842

PIGOTT Charles. *Jockey Club: a sketch of the manners of the age.* 2nd ed. (1792-3)

POLLOCK Mary. *History of Stockbridge races.* Talk given to the Hampshire Society 28th November 2001 and published on http://www.communigate.co.uk/hants/somsoc/page8.phtml

POND W. Sporting kalendar. (1751-72)

PORTER John. *John Porter of Kingsclere: an autobiography.* Grant Richards. (1919)

PORTER John. *Kingsclere.* Chatto Windus. (1896)

POWYS Caroline Lybbe. *Passages from the diaries of Mrs Philip Lybbe Powys 1756-1808.* ed E. J. Climenson. Longmans. (1899)

PRYOR Francis Rev. *Berkshire bachelor's diary being the diary and letters of Francis Pryor, recusant and gentleman farmer of Ufton, Berks, in the latter half of the 18th century.* Blacket Turner. Newbury (1936)

Racing Calendar 1773-

RANGER Paul. *Catalogue of strolling companies: ongoing theatre in Newbury.* Newbury District Museum. (1990)

Reading Mercury 1725-

Reading races or the Berkshire beauties (anon poem) Carnan Smart. Reading (1777)

ROBERTS Cecil. *And so to Bath.* Hodder. (1940)

ROCQUE John. Topographical survey of the county of Berks in 18 sheets. (1761)

ROSEVEAR Alan. *Coach and waggon services across the upper Thames valley.* Roads across the upper Thames valley series 11 Wantage (1993)

RUNCIMAN J. 'Ethics of the turf.' *Contemporary Review* (1889) p607-8

SCARTH-DIXON William. *South Berks Hunt.* Hunt Clubs Association. (1922)

SCARTH-DIXON William. *Vine Hunt.* Hunt Clubs Association. (1922)

SELWYN David. *Poetry of Jane Austen and the Austen family.* University of Iowa Press. (1997)

SETH-SMITH Michael et al. *History of steeplechasing.* Joseph. (1966)

Sporting Life

Sporting Magazine 1793-.

Sporting sketches 6 Oct 1905.

STAWELL Jessica. *History of Burford and Bibury racecourse.* Tolsey Papers no3. Burford (1980)

STAWELL Jessica. *Burford and Bibury racecourses: a history.* Hindsight of Burford. (2000)

STEINMETZ Andrew. *Gaming table: its votaries and victims.* (1870)

Stockbridge Races 17-19th June 1863 poster Hampshire Record Office. 31M51

SUFFOLK AND BERKSHIRE Henry Charles Howard earl of. *Racing and steeplechasing.* (1886)

TATE W. E. *Domesday of English enclosure acts and awards.* University of Reading. (1978)

TAUNTON Thomas. *Famous horses.* Sampson Low (nd)

The Times.

THOMPSON F. M. L. *Rise of respectable society.* Fontana. (1988)

THOMPSON F. M. L. *Cambridge social history of Britain 1750-1950.* CUP. (1990)

THORMANBY. *Kings of the Turf.* Hutchinson. (1898)

TOLSON John & VAMPLEW Wray. 'Derailed: railways and horse racing revisited.' *Sports Historian* 18 (2) Nov 98 p34-50

TOMALIN Claire. *Jane Austen.* Penguin. (2000)

Truth as opposed to fiction or an authentic and impartial review of the life of the late Rt Hon the Earl of Barrymore. (1793)

TURBERVILLE A. S. ed. *Johnson's England.* Clarendon. Oxford (1933)

TYRREL John. *Racecourses on the flat.* Crowood. (1989)

VAMPLEW Wray. *Turf :a social and economic history of horse racing.* Allen Lane. (1976)

Victoria County History Berkshire. IHR. (1907)

Victoria County History Hampshire. IHR. (1912)

Victoria County History Oxfordshire. IHR. (1907)

Victoria County History Wiltshire.IHR. (1959)

WALFORD Edwards. *County families of the United Kingdom.* Hardwicke. (1889)

West Berkshire Museum. Racing file and Bundle 2004.7.Racecourse

WHITE John. *Racegoer's encyclopaedia.* Collins Willow. (1994)

Who was who 1897-1915. A & C Black. (1988)

WHYTE, James Christie. *History of the British turf.* Colburn. (1840)

WILLIAMS Alfred. *Villages of the White Horse.* Duckworth. (1913)

WINTLE William. *Compton and East Ilsley: a comparative study of two Berkshire parishes in the nineteenth century.* University of Oxford dissertation. (2001)

WOODFORDE James Rev. *Diary of a country parson.* ed John Beresford. vol iv 1793-96. Clarendon. (1929)

WOODWARD George Rev. *Parson in the Vale of the White Horse: letters from East Hendred 1753-1761.* ed. Donald Gibson. Sutton. Stroud (1982)

Index